- Praise for The

"I wish I had read this book twenty-five years ago because I wouldn't have made the mistakes I did and ruined my life."
Anonymous male, 45

Philippa McSkimming, Regional General Nurse, Midwifery— Mum and Survivor
I recommend this book to anyone who is unsure or suffering in their relationship. It's a best friend. An insightful book, which speaks the truth about our emotions in a way that leaves the reader empowered.

Dr Andrew McCauley, Consultant Psychiatrist
You may think this is a frightening book; the title suggests that it is a strident feminist rant. In fact, it is nothing of the sort and you will find it to be a refreshing, realistic guide to a crisis that affects many. The authors emphasise this point themselves, by saying they are not a man-bashing book, and they haven't done that and there is much here that is relevant to anybody and everybody facing a relationship crisis.

In Chapter One the telltale signs are listed, followed by 'your reaction to the truth' in Chapter Two. Other themes include grief and understanding the adulterer. This in particular, is very important and I thought the authors were spot on with the points they made. The book is not prescriptive but makes many practical suggestions for you to consider. I did like the guidance on what is required if you are going to rebuild your relationship. The Reconciliation

Script would be helpful for the man to read and I believe the authors are in the process of writing a book for men who have been betrayed too.

It is easy to feel overwhelmed at times like this. This book will help make sense of some of the options you have and perhaps have not considered. In the Chapter on 'Self Inflicted Pain', the line 'the responsibility for any continuing pain lies with you', is such an empowering thought if the pain is used correctly. The MAN*Script* shows you how to do this as well as other practical suggestions.

Alongside the book is My Freedom Diary, which is an excellent tool in guiding and helping a woman through the process of recovery. By the end of which, the aim is for the betrayed woman to be able to hold her head up high and shine—Chapter 14 of The MAN*Script*.

The authors wanted to write an easy to read, reference and support guide; they have. I have no hesitation in recommending The MAN*Script* to my patients and any woman who is going through the emotional crisis of betrayal. This book clearly has its place in the 'life *script*' of being cheated on.

Dr Christine Howard, Consultant Paediatrician MBChB MRCPCH
As a UK National Health Service Consultant I am used to stuffy textbooks and psychology infused self-help books but when I picked up The MANScript, I read it in a morning! It is an accessible easy read, which is very relevant and insightful. This is a book for women written by women; full of real life scenarios.

If you are dealing with the hurt and guilt of betrayal, the

overwhelming message of the book is; "this is not your fault." This book is empowering for women. However, this is not a man-bashing book. It delves deeper into understanding the reasons men state for their infidelity and the *script* they often use to justify their actions. Any woman reading The MAN*Script* will identify with this and realise they are not alone in their experiences. It sets out a framework for women and a way forward for themselves, their partners, and importantly their children.

My favourite quote is, "You have the power." Every woman reading this book will feel empowered.

Dr Patel, Medical Director, Berkshire Primary Care
There is much more to this book than simply self-help. Its range is what I must congratulate, from gentle comfort and a kindly ear to a well researched, balanced source of information and a ready access to both the authors' professional expertise, which can all be used as a springboard to areas of deeper psychology and healing.

Betrayal is horrific and its aftermath can leave a legacy of mistrust and anxiety that destroys lives. In this book, there is a robust attempt to provide genuine support. It is not always sugar coated, but then real life is not a fairy tale and unfortunately, we do not always live happily ever after.

The writing and overall feel of this book is at once calming but with a breadth of deep feeling that also seems to convey detached expertise. As a doctor, the Holy Grail of consultation is empathy with a credible balance, to remain detached and unbiased but also to deeply care, which this book expertly achieves.

It provides an excellent, balanced view of betrayal and the very damaging human costs, as well as featuring the possible causes and various paths taken. The authors, I feel, are also at pains to remind the reader that there is a level of uncertainty and contrariness that exists, how very human.

For me, the winning approach is that this book works on a variety of levels for the readers who may be at very different stages on their difficult journey. This is the real beating heart of the book and which I feel has taken considered skill to write and provide, to help other people. It is very accessible and the real world examples, talking heads, and of course the painful experiences described, gives it a continued sense of verisimilitude.

Rather than detract, the prose is often laced with the urgency and first person feelings that can only be possessed by one who has lived and breathed the betrayal.

For some people, this book will be a manual, a guide and an invaluable aid to survival in the first instant. For other people, some way into their journey or beyond, it can offer so much more. With the added, perhaps unique offer of a direct link to the authors, this will most certainly enable a wider discussion of the hidden depths to many of the ideas that permeate throughout infidelity and betrayal. It is here that the book reveals its true strength.

Bella Stringfellow, wife of British businessman, nightclub owner, Peter Stringfellow
I think this book is exactly the comfort a woman needs who has been cheated on. It will help them make the first step into recovering from their ordeal. I think it's very professional and

covers every emotion you go through. Plus, the excuses men give are such an eye opener that I think women will want to read it even if they haven't been cheated on!

Anne Marie Curtis, Registered Nurse
There is currently a distinct lack of support and literature to support women facing betrayal in their relationship. This book will without doubt give great comfort, help and hope to anyone going through what is the most upsetting and challenging time of their lives. It totally validates how a person feels when they have been betrayed.

The messages in this book are clear and it is incredibly supportive. This book is clearly written from the heart with a genuine warmth, understanding and a desire to enable those who have been betrayed to move forward in a positive way.

From an adulterous male, who sadly wants to remain anonymous
For the first time ever, I could actually understand what I had put my wife through. I feel utterly ashamed not only at what I did but that I didn't for one minute grasp the damage I had caused her. I am so proud of her for the person she has become, despite all that I did to her.

The MANScript

Julia Keys AND Jacqui Coles

Hashtag PRESS

This edition published in Great Britain by Hashtag Press 2018

Text copyright © Julia Keys and Jacqueline Coles 2018
Copyright Cover illustration © Helen Braid 2018

A CIP catalogue for this book is available from the British Library.

ISBN 978-1-9998053-3-3

Typeset in Garamond Classic 11.25/14 by Blaze Typesetting

Printed in Great Britain by Clays Ltd, St Ives plc

Hashtag PRESS

HASHTAG PRESS BOOKS
Hashtag Press Ltd
Kent, England, United Kingdom
Email: info@hashtagpress.co.uk
Website: www.hashtagpress.co.uk
Twitter: @hashtag_press

In loving memory of my parents, Jack and Cath Clark. To my children—Josh and Jemma—and with thanks for all the support from my wonderful friends and family.
- Julia -

With love to John for all the support and encouragement you gave Julia and I, whilst we were writing this book. To my family for always being there, especially in the tough times.
- Jacqui -

Acknowledgements

Hashtag Press—Helen and Abiola, thank you for publishing the book and making it a reality for us. Helen Braid for her amazing cover design and innovative ideas. Kate Turner for her fabulous skills that have made the inside of the book as beautiful as the outside.

Literally PR—To Helen and the team at Literally PR.

Wendy Yorke—Literary Agent, Editor and Author Coach—Thank you for taking us on and for supporting us through our journey.

Our Beta Readers—Dr Andrew McCauley, Dr Christine Howard, Dr Prash Patel, Philippa McSkimming, Anne-Marie Curtis and Bella Stringfellow.

We can't thank you enough for taking the time to read our book. Your personal professional contributions and assessments have helped us enormously.

Chris and Stephanie Lewis—Thank you for lending us your beautiful apartment in Majorca, which gave us the time and space to write this book.

Shirley Palmer at Shirley Palmer International—Thank you for guiding us through the labyrinth of the business world.

The names of individuals whose stories are shared in this book, have been changed to protect their identity, but their experiences are all true and we thank them all for being brave enough to share their stories with us. So many women contributed to The MAN*Script* and we thank them for their strength and courage in sharing their experiences with us, so that we can all help other women. We know many of them are still struggling with the impact of what happened to them, which makes their contributions even more brave.

During our research, several men agreed to tell us why they had affairs and what they did. It was the first time all of them had actually spoken about what they had done and they provided us with very candid accounts of their betrayal. We thank them for their honesty.

We would also thank all the London taxi drivers who unwittingly got more than they bargained for, with our questions enquiring if they had ever cheated on their partner!

Special thanks to our families and friends for all their loyal support, without which, neither of us would have been able to write The MAN*Script*.

Contents of The MAN*Script*

- How to deal with the changes in your life
- Feel, manage and repair the pain
- Remember. . .

Chapter Five: His Own *Script*
- Men's interpretations of their *scripts* in their own words
- Alan's story (and *script*)
- Chris's story (and *script*)
- Tom's story (and *script*)
- What have Alan, Chris and Tom got in common?

Chapter Six: His Other-Woman *Script*
- How far men will go to protect the Other-Woman
- Jeff's story (and *script*)
- Alan's response to *why*?
- Chris' response to *why*?
- The *script* he will tell you and the Other-Woman when he wants to reconcile your relationship
- Julia's story
- Magda's story
- A word of advice for the Other-Woman
- Remember. . .

Chapter Seven: Understand The Adulterer
- Why men cheat
- Understand the adulterer's mind
- The sixty-six-million-dollar question, "Will he change?"

"No one makes you feel inferior without your consent."

Eleanor Roosevelt
American politician, diplomat and activist, 1884-1962

Introduction

There are many books published about how to deal with the aftermath of an affair, whether it is in the form of reconciliation or moving on.

The MAN*Script* is different.

It provides, for the first time, the information about *what* men say and what men *do* when they are cheating on their partner, so that you can both understand and deal with your emotions, and ultimately make the best decisions for your joint futures—together or apart.

The MAN*Script* is designed to you help you. . .
- Have the confidence to say how you feel, in the hope of bringing about a form of communication, which will facilitate a resolution to the conflict you feel.
- Know you are not on your own with your feelings.
- Feel stronger again when you are at your most vulnerable.
- Gain the tools to stay focussed on what is real.
- Understand that whatever the outcome of your suspicions, you can survive and be happy.

At every stage of betrayal, communication is the key to saving your relationship or moving on.

The MAN*Script* is designed to bring your attention to the various *scripts* that men use when cheating. Armed with this knowledge, you will be more able to talk about your suspicions in a calm and appropriate manner. By asking questions early and communicating your concerns with your partner, you are opening the door to an opportunity to discuss the worries you both may have.

This book will guide you through all the emotions you feel, from that initial twinge of suspicion to potentially dealing with the pain and grief at the loss of a relationship. It will support you on your own personal journey, to reassure you that you are not 'going mad' and to validate how you are feeling.

There is a focus on emotions within The MAN*Script* for the simple reason that it is your emotions that will influence your choices of how you deal with being cheated on. Unless you understand your feelings and know what to do with them, you are going to be vulnerable when making choices that may not be the best for you and your family. We want you to be in the strongest mindset possible when it comes to the big decisions that you face.

The MAN*Script* is written from both personal and professional experience. Jacqui and Julia know what it feels like to be betrayed and they also know what help a woman needs when they have been cheated on.

Asking for help can be one of the hardest things to do when you suspect or discover that you have been betrayed. It can feel like one of the loneliest places on earth. Finding someone trustworthy who won't judge or get fed up with you, and importantly, keep your confidence, can be difficult. Knowing what you are feeling is normal will give you the confidence to know you are not going mad, you're not alone, and there is a way out of this feeling.

The MAN*Script* will help you understand and manage your emotions if you. . .

- Have reason to feel suspicious about your partner's behaviour.
- Have found out that your partner has been cheating on you.
- Are struggling to cope.
- Feel as though you are losing your mind (or you are being told that by your partner).
- Are feeling lonely and alone.
- Are feeling shame about your partner's cheating.
- Need help to deal with your thoughts and feelings.
- Are feeling guilty and are taking responsibility for your partner's actions.
- Are being blamed for your partner's behaviour.
- Are stuck with decisions about what to do next.
- Want to maintain your dignity and self-esteem.
- Need help to move on.
- Are saying to yourself, *"How could he do this to me?"*

Alongside The MAN*Script*, the My Freedom Diary has been designed to help free yourself from the emotional pain of betrayal. It's a day-by-day, step-by-step guide to get you through the hurtful times, into a space of feeling happy and empowered.

Introduction by Julia Keys

"The gap between where we are and where we want to be
is only a thought away."
Julia Keys, 2018

If you have picked up this book we suspect you are curious, or have some doubts, about your own relationship. If you have been cheated on by your partner, you will be familiar with the tell-tale signs and we hope reading this book will help you understand that it is not your fault. Instead, you have been MAN*Scripted*.

Throughout this book, we are very clear that it is a person's choice to have an affair and that applies to both men and women. Jacqui and I want to emphasise that without communication in a relationship, there is no opportunity for you or your partner to put right what may be wrong.

This is when regrets can kick in and you may find yourself looking back and wishing you had done certain things; had more sex or shown him more love. Whatever your regret might be, if your partner had talked before taking the decision to have an affair, maybe it could have been prevented.

That is why we say it is not your fault if your partner chooses to have an affair and not talk to you. We strongly encourage you to talk, talk, talk—about any problems you have—in the hope that you can avoid the pain of betrayal.

If he can communicate what was wrong with your relationship as an excuse for cheating, then he could have told you before he was tempted to cross the line.

Some men have said this book is 'too accurate to publish.' Other men have been extremely supportive—surprisingly, many are men who have had an affair—while other men, the naysayers, have used words such as 'dispirited', 'distasteful', and 'offensive.' We think you probably get the picture.

One man told us that this sort of thing shouldn't even be talked about. "Why do women have to tell everyone when they have been cheated on?"

It is the same old *script*.

"I can cheat on you but don't tell anyone."

No! It doesn't work like that. You need to talk and find support. If men find it distasteful or offensive that you are choosing to not feel alone or unsupported, then the message to them is simple. Stop cheating.

What I do want to be clear about, is that Jacqui and I are not writing a man-bashing book. The MAN*Script* has been written to help all women who have been cheated on and who have gone through the painful process of betrayal.

We tell unfaithful women the same message as we tell men. You 'chose' to have an affair, it is not something you were 'made' to do. In fact, sometimes men who have been cheated on, may find it harder to deal with the issue, than women.

Many of the men we spoke to told us that it is was their ego, plus the fact that they don't like to be left on their own, that made it difficult to accept rejection, alongside their desire to *save face*. Some went as far as saying they told their mates, "I was going to dump her anyway."

We hope any man reading The MAN*Script* will learn something from it as well. Ironically, my husband did when he read the first draft of the book. He told me that he could see himself in every *script* and that was when he realised the writing was on the wall for the affair he was having. The MAN*Script* made him wake up to what he was losing and what a fool he had been. However, it was only when we finally went to court, making the situation real, that the full impact of his affair hit him.

For the past seventeen years working as a therapist, I have supported women, men and families whose worlds have fallen apart because of infidelity. The impact is enormous and reverberates further than the couple, and the need for support is huge. This support was not always easy to come by, which is why Jacqui and I developed the website, www. keys2life.co.uk, to provide help and encouragement for those people who need it.

The majority of women we speak to say their main and only support has been friends, usually more so than family. In many cases, they kept the pain and anguish hidden from their loved ones.

There is a fear of being judged by other people (and sometimes concern about the partner being judged). The fear of being viewed as a failure has been their primary motivation for keeping the situation a secret. This can lead some susceptible women into isolation, depression and anxiety.

There is one word that sums up the feelings you have after finding out you have been cheated on and that is *excruciating*. It can be so damaging to women, yet infidelity is the elephant in the room. It happens all the time, but for some women there is a reluctance to talk about it, or acknowledge it, mainly because of shame.

How a woman deals with the impact of an affair can

significantly impact her self-esteem, her health and that of her friends, family and children, if applicable.

Why is it that a woman can carry the burden of that shame when it is her partner who should be the shameful one? Feelings of shame can lead to poor mental and physical health, panic attacks, and loss of confidence. Experts believe it can cause Post Traumatic Stress Disorder (PTSD).

One thing is for sure; unwanted images, irrational thoughts, emotional numbness, fear, a fogged mind, an inability to sleep and unpredictable explosions of anger and/or uncontrollable sobbing, can overwhelm every woman who has been betrayed. A woman can also become totally obsessed with wanting to know the truth and become a super-vigilant, amateur detective and forensic investigator.

In the following chapters, we have included some of the common signs and traits that men display, when they are being unfaithful. Cheating requires a capacity to lie and deceive to hide a secretive other life.

While writing this book with Jacqui, and since discovering my husband's infidelity, we realised there was a common theme emerging. The men who were having an affair seemed to be following a *script*. Not only were they saying similar things, but their behaviour was also very predictable. The same lies were being said to their partners and the same excuses were being used in an attempt to cover up their deceit and infidelity. My husband was also following the same *script* and that is how I caught him out.

The *scripts* appear to follow a pattern. There are *scripts* men follow before they are caught. There are *scripts* they adopt for themselves (his Own *Script*). There is the *script* for their partner;

the *script* they spin to the Other-Woman; and the *scripts* they tell your friends, their family and work colleagues.

In the following pages, we will take you through all the *scripts*. We have deliberately summarised the typical *scripts* at the beginning of the book. You don't have to search through all the pages to assure yourself that he is following a *script*. Later in the book, we include what men who cheat tell other people, but remember, men can behave very badly towards you, but they hate the idea of other people thinking badly of them.

The most important *script* that you need to know about, if you and your partner want to try and save your relationship, is the Reconciliation *Script*. This is the *script* that he must commit to, for you to have any chance of trusting him again. We discuss this in Chapter Eleven: The Reconciliation *Script*.

Many women have also told us that what they thought was 'real' had completely lost its reality. It is our hope that the words in this book will empower women to recover themselves and not lose sight of their own identity.

As women, we can also inflict excruciating pain on ourselves by taking the blame for our partner's actions. Many women follow a self-blame *script*. By doing this, we deflect the responsibility away from our partner and give him the perfect justification for his actions.

We have deliberately repeated some messages about looking after yourself and not taking the blame. This is imperative to your recovery. We want to keep reminding you that it was your partner's choice to have an affair, that you did not 'make' him do it and that it is not your fault; he made that choice.

You deserve to be valued and respected.

You will see throughout the pages of the book we do not

use the word *humiliated*. Many women use this word to explain how they feel after discovering their partner's affair. We don't use it because it is not you who should be humiliated. It is your partner and the Other-Woman. They are the ones who should be humiliated by the way they have behaved. If you are one of those women, who is feeling humiliated, STOP RIGHT NOW!

Writing The MAN*Script* was something Jacqui and I felt compelled to do for a long time. When we are in the emotional pain that follows betrayal, we can lose sight of who we really are and we can think that we have no control over our emotions and actions. We literally go into survival mode. We want to show women that there is always hope, despite how you might feel when it happens to you.

Not all women have access to support from friends or therapists. By reading this book, Jacqui and I hope it will provide you with the information and support you need to help you move forward in a positive and constructive manner.

Knowing your partner is following the same *script* as other men will empower you to see how unimaginative a man who cheats really is. Information gives a person power. It enables you to make decisions, which keep you safe and reduce your vulnerability. Our main aim in this book is to give the power back to you.

According to http://www.illicitentencounters.com, a UK-based extramarital dating website, '*2016 saw the highest recorded number of people having extramarital affairs.*'

This increase in affairs emphasises how important it is to be informed.

There are many self-help books written about how to improve your self-esteem and make your life positive. These books can be very wordy and as Jacqui and I know, the last thing many women are able to do when suspecting or discovering their partner's affair, is to focus on and absorb the vast amount of information these books contain. That is why this book is written as an easy-read, reference and support guide. Moreover, it has been written specifically for you and not just as a general life improvement guide.

Knowledge is power. It enables you to make decisions, which help to keep you safe and reduce your vulnerability. Our main aim is to give you an insight into the words and actions that an adulterer may use, so you can be one step ahead. If you start reading this book while asking yourself, "How *could* he do this to me?" We hope by the end of the book you will be saying instead, "How *dare* he do this to me?"

Julia x

After the final divorce hearing and ironically coinciding with the completion of The MAN*Script*, Julia's husband, Richard Keys, gave this quote: "I deeply regret the day I ever got involved in an affair and hurt my wife and family so much. If I had one wish it would be to turn the clock back and we would be together now. I will never give up on that hope."

Richard added a note of warning for any man thinking about having an affair: "If you really love your wife but are tempted to get a bit of excitement elsewhere—you have to be prepared to lose the one you really love—it just isn't worth it."

A message from Jacqui

It doesn't matter if you are fifteen or fifty; when it comes to dealing with the emotions and fallout of betrayal we all feel the same heartache. Even when we think we have moved on from betrayal, the impact can lay buried for years, only to return and catch you off your guard when you least expect it.

Emma Thompson has revealed that she called upon the experience of her own heartbreak to play a jilted wife in the 2003 film, *Love Actually*. We all remember the scene where her character, Karen, finds jewellery that her husband has bought for another woman and she breaks down in tears. We also refer to that scene later in the book. Yes, Emma Thompson is a great Oscar-winning actress, but it was her own experiences that made that scene, one that not many of us got through without shedding tears.

She later said, "That scene, where my character is standing by the bed crying, is so well known because it's something everyone's been through."

Like many of you, I fully understand how she felt. Although it was a long time ago for me, I remember when I was so in love with a man who betrayed me not once, but twice, I thought I would never get over it.

Watching Julia go through her heartbreak, over the last two years, has brought back memories that I thought had long ago faded. It surprised me how vivid they were. I saw what Julia was going through and actually relived it all again with her.

I know Julia will agree that this has been one of the most

challenging and demanding times in her life. Dealing with a very public betrayal, as well as having to stay strong for those who depend on her, has taken all her strength and fortitude.

Standing by Julia's side, I realised that although my own memories were still able to take me by surprise (I would be lying if I said I didn't shed some tears), I realised how that experience made me a stronger person. I made a pact with myself that never again would I allow anyone to walk all over me and take me for a fool. As much as it was devastating and hurtful at the time, it is probably one of the most important experiences I have had in life. It helped me become the person I am today.

I realised a long time ago that there comes a point when you have to focus on yourself and let go of the painful memories. To forgive does not mean you are saying it's OK, or you accept the affair, but for me, forgiveness means you are releasing yourself from the shackles of bitterness and resentment, and believe me bitterness is a very tight shackle! However, once you are released, you are free to live your life on your terms, without carrying their life around with you.

Bitterness can be so consuming, it can even show in your face. Remember, you attract more bees with nectar than you do with vinegar, so no matter how hard it is, try to set yourself free from the burden of the bitterness.

In both my professional career and personal life, I have supported so many women who believed at the time of finding out about their partner's affair that they would never survive. They never thought that eventually they would thrive. Those who have been able to let go and focus on themselves have certainly thrived. You never recover from betrayal by travelling in a straight line, so you have to accept there will be bad days as well as good, but always look forward.

I know Julia was determined not to let the past cloud the present to the point where the future appeared out of reach. She regularly said to me, "I have got to keep looking forward Jac, I've just got to keep looking forward." This was so important to her that we have put it on every other page of our My Freedom Diary, along with the words 'I matter,' because frankly, you do.

I do not, for one minute, diminish how hard or challenging it is. Some days it's as though you are totally stuck, others it's two steps forward and one back, but each day those steps will be stronger. I know that one day you will look back, like me, and realise it gave you the chance to walk your own path, that's even if you stay with your partner.

Sometimes good people do bad things, but a relationship with healthy foundations can heal and may even be better. You can go on to have great relationships, whether it's with the partner who betrayed you or in a new relationship. You will know what is right for *you*. So, it's onwards and upwards, girls!

Together, Julia and I wrote The MAN*Script* and by doing that, we have both moved forward. We know there are many women out there (and men) who have gone through the same experience as us and we hope we can be an example to you.

At the same time, we really want men who have betrayed their partner to know that it is not only in the moment that a woman is affected, in some capacity the impact of that betrayal will last a life-time.

For those women who knowingly get involved with a man who is already in a relationship (we know some of you are duped by their lies) you are betraying another woman. Ask yourself this, "How would I feel if this was my man?"

I am so proud that Julia not only survived, but thrived and with our help, you can too.

We are all in this together.

Jacqui x

The Typical MAN*Scripts*

As well as the obvious tell-tale signs that are listed below, these are the typical *scripts* that men will tell people around him, including you, himself, the Other-Woman, and family, friends and colleagues. This also includes the Reconciliation *Script*, which are the rules you must set for him to follow. Throughout this book we refer to his mistress or the affair partner as the Other-Woman.

The tell-tale signs
- Your gut instinct.
- His changing behaviour.
- He stops noticing you.
- Signs of sexual activity.
- His appearance.
- He becomes secretive about his mobile telephone, tablet/laptop and emails.
- He spends less time at home.
- He is increasingly late home from work /gym.
- He shows less interest in having sex with you.
- He talks about the Other-Woman.

When he has been 'found out'
It's your fault (of course!)
We could write an entire book about the excuses men tell and the blame they fire at us women! Men who cheat are masters of re-writing history to suit themselves. But before we tell you what the most common excuses are, here are a selection of jaw

dropping, real-life quotations from men we spoke to during the research for this book.

- "It was a lack of oxygen to my brain that made me not realise what I was doing!"
- "I swear to you, since the day we married, I have never once taken off my wedding ring. I just happened not to have it on in that photo."
- "I don't know how she got pregnant with my baby because I have never had sex with her."
- "I never wanted to hurt you, I just didn't expect to get caught."
- "She categorically was not in our flat; that underwear has to be yours."
- "I was so shocked when you told me that she had put a picture on Facebook showing she was in the same hotel as me. I left straight away before she realised I was there too. It was a close shave!"
- "I deny everything only because I don't want to hurt you by telling you the truth."
- "You psychologically willed me to have an affair so you could be proved right."
- "I bought her the engagement ring she is wearing as a goodbye gift because I felt sorry for her!"
- "I had no idea she was going to be in Trinidad at the same time as me, what a coincidence!"

If you would like to share the most jaw-dropping excuses you have been told, please contact us via our website: www. keys2life.co.uk.

Typical male excuses

- You were not there for me when I needed you to listen to me.
- You spend more time talking to your friends than me.
- You only have time for the children leaving me feeling frozen out.
- You put everyone else before me.
- You are obsessed with your job.
- You spend too much money.
- You drink too much.
- You don't look after yourself; you are a mess.
- You don't let me anywhere near you.
- You don't show me affection.
- We never have sex.
- You don't understand me.
- You told me it was over between us.
- It's all in your head.

His justification

- I didn't plan it, it just happened.
- I thought you didn't love me.
- It was a fantasy that wasn't real; it was a bit of fun and excitement.
- Everyone does it.
- I was drunk.
- It only happened once *(it rarely does)*.
- A man has needs.
- I felt guilty all the time, as I was really thinking about you.
- I have learnt my lesson and will never do it again.
- I've learnt my lesson and I have changed.

- I was stupid and wasn't thinking straight.
- It is in my genes, there is nothing I can do about it!

It's not what it seems
- I love *you*.
- I don't want to lose you.
- She is just a friend.
- She means nothing to me.
- I don't know anything about her, really.
- I don't even know where she lives.
- It is not what it looks like.

His Own *Script*
- No one will find out.
- I won't get caught.
- She will be grateful, because I won't be asking her for sex.
- What she doesn't know can't hurt her.
- It's just a physical thing.
- I deserve the thrill of an affair because my life is otherwise miserable.

His Other-Woman *Script*
What he tells the Other-Woman
- She doesn't understand me.
- We live separate lives.
- We haven't had sex for a long time.
- I don't love her anymore.
- There is no romantic connection between us anymore.
- We are more like brother and sister.
- We are only together for the children.

- You are the most gorgeous woman I have ever known.
- I love you.
- I am going to leave her for you.
- She has betrayed me.

His Other People *Script*

- It is not what it seems.
- She has got it all wrong.
- My life has been very difficult for a long time.
- We live totally separate lives.
- She has betrayed me; had an affair, is an alcoholic; or spent all my money.
- She told me our relationship/marriage was finished, so that is why I continued the affair.
- People are stirring up trouble and saying things that aren't true.

The Reconciliation *Script*

He must:

- Have absolutely no contact with the Other-Woman.
- Accept the Other-Woman no longer exists in his life.
- Allow you to distrust him.
- Show you how much you matter to him.
- Not show anger or frustration when you question him and show a lack of trust.
- Take actions that speak louder than his words.
- Be prepared to talk openly to you and answer your questions.
- Have patience; rebuilding trust takes a very long time.
- Earn your forgiveness.

"There were three of us in this marriage, so it was a bit crowded."

Diana Princess of Wales,
1961–1997

Chapter One

The Tell-Tale Signs

We are going to describe the words and behaviours used by many men when they are cheating. We will help you to find out what he is up to! There may be other clues unique to your partner that only you, as the person closest to him, find suspicious. We explore how you are likely to react to your suspicions and we help you understand your reaction rather than fear it. Remember, it is a normal response to finding out the truth.

His denial

Almost always, a partner caught cheating will at first deny it. In fact, if your partner has cheated on you, almost certainly he won't tell you. If you have a suspicion and you confront him, he probably won't admit it. Even when you have the hard evidence the likelihood is that he still won't admit it!

However, there is more hope for your relationship if he does admit to the affair than if he doesn't. No relationship can be reconciled with continuing lies and denial.

The list of tell-tale signs included previously aren't necessarily proof in isolation, but they are very common to many men who cheat. The days of simply looking for lipstick on the collar are long gone, although some women have told us it is how they first found out!

Technology has given us many opportunities and the tools to catch a cheating man, but the one thing that will guide you above all else, is your gut instinct.

Your instinct

Trust your gut feeling, sixth sense or whatever you want to call it, because this is a very powerful instinct. If you have suspicions ask yourself, *why do I have I these suspicions?*

You may not have absolute proof, but sometimes you simply know. You feel it. Trust the voice deep inside you. Remember your gut instinct is your partner's worst nightmare because it means you are on to him.

Of course, he will do everything he can to create self-doubt. Do not allow your instinct to be challenged, otherwise you are on the road to not trusting yourself, something that can come so easily with betrayal.

Often it can be the tone of his voice or subtle changes in the person you thought you knew so well. Something starts to niggle you. It can be very basic, like finding a receipt for flowers or jewellery you never received, or an increase in sudden or frequent late-night texts.

They are the obvious signs, but some men are better than others at deceit. Despite this, even the most deceptive men make a mistake in the end; take your time and be patient. Once you have suspicions and then evidence that he is unaware of, you are in control of the situation.

To be a good liar you have to have a good memory and sooner or later he will slip up and you will get your proof.

How many times have you heard someone say, "I wish I had listened to my gut instinct. I just had a feeling something wasn't right?"

Don't go making any life-changing decisions based on gut instinct alone, instead use it as a reason to dig deeper and find concrete evidence of him MAN*Scripting* you. You know him better than anyone and you know when he is lying to you.

Let us be clear about this, we are not saying that all women in relationships should become Miss Marple. On the contrary, we are saying that if you feel suspicious, it is likely that you have a reason to feel like that.

Throughout this book you will see that we encourage you to communicate your thoughts and feelings to your partner, so that there is an opportunity for you both to discuss your worries in the hope of developing, not destroying your relationship.

In fact, talking through your suspicions would be seen as a chance to stop the rot before it happens. However, we do understand that when you see something that makes you suspicious and gut feeling comes into play, it is so very hard to ignore things and not act on it. The most important thing is to do what is right for you.

So many women have told us how they just knew something wasn't right and became obsessed with finding out the truth, for example, tracking their husband's car journeys.

Debbie, a forty-two-year-old teacher from Birmingham, couldn't ignore her gut instinct and started following her husband everywhere he went, even on a bicycle. Her bike had previously sat in the shed for six years, so she was super fit by the time she got her evidence!

Debbie said, "I had to find out the truth, because it was

driving me mad. One thing he would never have expected to find me on was a bike."

Anne, a thirty-five-year-old nurse and mother of two from New Zealand, told us how she tracked her husband on his mobile and made her way to the town she knew he was in. She asked the taxi driver to drop her off near the restaurant she had him located him in.

As the taxi pulled up, her husband was standing outside the restaurant. She panicked when she saw him, but she needn't have worried because as she got out of the taxi he was so engrossed with the Other-Woman, he hadn't realised his own wife was standing right next to him!

Anne was wearing a new coat he had recently bought her, but it clearly made her invisible. Conversely, she had seen the messages her husband had sent to his Other-Woman every day, obsessed with asking her what she was wearing, even down to the colour dress she had on!

One of the replies she saw was, 'My dress is grey, like the weather and my day without you.'

When we asked women about what made them think their partners were cheating on them, they typically said first, "I just knew."

Changes in his behaviour

He may become very aggressive and critical towards you, clearly irritated by you and what you do or don't do. Many men deflect their guilt by picking arguments or justifying their actions by giving themselves an excuse for their behaviour. For example, "We are always arguing. We don't get on. I can never do anything right for you." Sound familiar?

It is far easier on the conscience to cheat on a partner you constantly argue with than one who is kind and loving. He will make himself feel better by telling himself that this is why he had to turn to someone else. Try to stay calm and don't take the bait. It is not your fault. We know how hard and frightening it is to deal with what can be his immense anger towards you and we discuss this in Chapter Thirteen: Moving On.

If you start questioning him he may become angry, accusing you of not trusting him. When faced with this, we often doubt our own instincts and begin to question ourselves. Remember, attacking you is the best line of his defence.

The most important thing is to keep yourself safe. By this, we mean if you feel at all scared or threatened by your partner's behaviour, you must remove yourself from the situation immediately and call someone to support you. His anger is with himself and there are instances when women have been attacked by men to deflect from their own guilt.

In the United States, over half of the killings of American women are related to intimate partner violence, with the vast majority of the victims dying at the hands of a current or former romantic partner, according to a report released by the Centers for Disease Control and Prevention in 2017.

Some men go to the other extreme and are so consumed with guilt they start buying you flowers and gifts—trying almost too hard. Being overly nice to throw you off the scent is another tell-tale sign, although it is not as common as anger.

He stops noticing you

Some men who are cheating seem to be so preoccupied that they hardly notice you're there. He may avoid contact with you and doesn't call you as much during the day as he once did. Even when you make an effort to look your best, he doesn't notice what you are wearing or acknowledge how nice you look.

During conversations, he may be distracted and not really be listening to what you say. He may daydream; spend time looking out of windows and seem to be distant with you.

He may stop confiding in you or stop telling you about his work. Although he is physically with you, emotionally his mind may be elsewhere.

Signs of sexual activity

Sorry girls, but stained underpants are one of the most obvious signs. If he has been working late or been out with his mates and comes home with stained underpants, you have to ask yourself why?

He may hide his underpants. If he is clever—or at least thinks he is clever—he will put a dirty pair of underpants back in the drawer and replace them with clean ones when you are in the bathroom! He'll solve that problem or at least attempt to do so by offering to do the washing at the weekend when he'll slip the dirty pair in with the rest of the load.

His appearance

He may suddenly start taking an interest in his appearance and buy new clothes, throwing out his faithful old boxers for new underwear.

Lydia, a fifty-three-year-old musician from Scotland, said, "My partner suddenly took an interest in fashion and wearing trendy clothes when he had never shown any interest in his appearance before. The skinny jeans he bought were so tight he could hardly walk—he looked ridiculous."

A sudden interest in going to the gym and wanting to look his best coinciding with the other tell-tale signs, can indicate he is trying to impress someone.

If he has been with the Other-Woman before coming home to you, he may shower before he goes to bed in an attempt to hide her smell and remove any feelings of guilt he may have.

Some men become very keen on cleaning their cars. This behaviour, suddenly out of the blue, usually signals that he is trying to make a good impression on someone, but more likely it might be a way of removing or checking for any evidence from his car, such as a strand of hair.

He becomes secretive about his mobile telephone and emails

This is not as easy as you may think. The unaccomplished cheat, the first-time or virgin cheater will make naïve and obvious mistakes. If he suddenly stops leaving his telephone around the place, puts a PIN or new PIN on it, it may suggest there is something on his telephone that he doesn't want you to see.

He may become secretive, edgy and sensitive about his telephone, placing it on silent and keeping it face down when he never used to before. He may start taking it everywhere with him, never letting it out of his sight.

He may hide her number in his telephone under a male name you don't recognise or as a male work colleague, probably one you have never heard of.

He might receive late night text messages, supposedly from his boss or a wrong number that he says wasn't meant for him.

If you look at his telephone the next day and the message or calls have been deleted, then something is not right. This sort of activity should start to raise your alarm bells.

This also applies to emails. If he is suddenly overly keen for you to read his emails, it can be a clue that he has another email account. As with his telephone, changing his email password and not allowing you to have it means he has something to hide.

Turning off his location services on his telephone and actually turning off his mobile, claiming he had no signal when you tried to get hold of him, is another clue. Of course, on occasions there will be poor signal coverage and black spots, but they rarely last for three hours or across several miles!

If he develops a weak bladder every time you are out together, the chances are he is going to the Gents to use his telephone. If you can check his bill, text messages and calls will often coincide with his frequent need to pee.

However, men who are accomplished cheaters will have another telephone hidden somewhere and be happy or even keen for you to look at their private and/or work telephones. When you first raise suspicions about his behaviour, he may actively encourage you to look at his telephone. He will leave his telephone laying around, displaying the 'Hey look at me, I have nothing to hide' attitude. This, combined with some of the other tell-tale signals, is usually a sign that he actually does have something to hide!

Polly, a thirty-year-old shop assistant from Canada, told us how she had found two secret phones over a six-month period. In the end, she put a very small tape recorder in her fiancé's coat pocket. She heard him go to a local phone box and call the Other-Woman.

She said, "He just couldn't stop himself and even when he knew I was hyper-vigilant and kept finding his phones, he resorted to a telephone box."

Finding a secret telephone can be tricky and takes time. Be patient, he will get clumsy and reveal where that telephone is; he will forget he has it with him or forget to hide it. This usually occurs when he may be drunk or under pressure. If not, his changed behaviour pattern can lead you to find out where he hides it in the end.

He spends less time at home

Suddenly he starts going out with his work colleagues more frequently and staying out late at night. He may have to start working away from home, sometimes for days at a time, when he didn't previously. This behaviour put together with the other clues can be a sign that he is cheating on you.

He shows less interest in having sex with you

Many of us believe that men can have sex without any emotional attachment, however this isn't always the case. It is quite common for men to show less interest in you sexually if he is having sex with someone else.

There are however, the men who carry on having sex with their partner, in fact want more, for fear that you may suspect them if they don't. Trust your gut instinct. You will know if it doesn't feel right.

He talks about 'her'

Believe it or not, men often give you the first clue about a woman they are cheating with or thinking about. They often start telling you about a female colleague they work with or know. He may start to use her name more frequently, be over helpful towards her and may even invite her into your home.

Esther, a forty-three-year-old dentist from France, who found out her husband was having an affair with an office colleague said, "My husband kept telling me about his new assistant in work and how much I would like her. He constantly mentioned her name, only now do I realise it's because he actually was so obsessed he couldn't stop thinking about her."

Friends or colleagues may give you clues

Never ignore what your friends or colleagues tell you. You may not want to hear or believe it about the person you love. It may even damage your friendships, but anyone who really cares about you will want you to know the truth.

Gut instinct, combined with what you are being told about your partner's sudden, friendly relationship with a work colleague or other female, shouldn't be ignored. If he becomes defensive when you ask him, he probably does have something to hide.

The most important thing to remember is to be patient. We know it is almost impossible. When you have your suspicions, it is natural to want to immediately confront your partner. We do not underestimate how hard this is, but you must remain patient.

If you confront him without having all your evidence, this usually ends up in an argument, with you being made to feel you are imagining things. By confronting him too soon, you are actually warning him and possibly making it harder to catch him with solid evidence.

This may seem contrary to what we have emphasised about the importance of communication, but if you are likely to confront him in anger it is best to wait. Again, trust your gut instinct, you know him better than anyone.

You may be in a relationship with one of the few men who immediately confess; these are rare. The majority of men will deny everything. What you are doing is giving him the excuse he needs to subsequently blame it on you and for him to say, "It's all your fault, because you were so jealous and suspicious of me." He may go on to say, "I couldn't cope with your insane suspicions and jealousy, so you pushed me away."

Be clever, be patient, you will get the evidence you need. Follow your gut instinct, tell trusted friends, but never warn him.

Men are creatures of habit and of the many women who contact us regularly the majority have found the evidence they need when their partner has been out of his comfort zone and normal routine. For example, he may have a secret place to hide his secret telephone. He is unlikely not to go on holiday with it, especially in the early stages of an affair with all the 'fun and excitement' he craves and is experiencing.

He will also need to constantly reassure the Other-Woman, who is probably fuming that he is away with you. This is your time to watch and pounce. While he is off guard, you need to be on guard, carefully watching his movements.

Sarah, a twenty-nine-year-old sales executive from Worcester, told us how she "just knew" by his actions from the minute they got to the airport on their way to a 'romantic' holiday. This has been common to many of the women who have contacted us. "I heard him say all the right words, but his actions didn't match his words."

Thirty-one-year-old Saariyah from South Africa explained that when she got home after a holiday to reconcile her relationship, she checked her partner's telephone bill and realised he had been calling and texting the Other-Woman, when she was in the shower.

Jess, a twenty-four-year-old beautician from Essex, found her fiancé's secret telephone on top of a wardrobe in their holiday apartment in France. She had her suspicions long before their holiday, which he had vehemently denied and told her it was all in her head.

She said, "I hid the telephone and never said a word to him. I could see him getting more and more agitated and anxious. He was trying to move the wardrobe and was rummaging through bags. In hindsight, it was quite comical to see him pretending to do push ups but actually checking under the bed to see if it was there. The anxiety he felt for those four days gave him a taste of what I felt for years.

"I think he thought he was losing his mind, he was unable to relax and clearly panicking. Of course, he couldn't ask me if I had seen it because after all it didn't exist. His Other-Woman obviously couldn't cope either and one night when we were sitting in the restaurant having a meal, the hotel manager came in and said there was a call for him from Sonia. I will never forget the look on his face, he suddenly lost his appetite, went very pale and wanted to be sick. I personally thought the food was lovely!"

Christmas is often another time to catch him off guard. During the festive period, most men are away from the office. If they want to keep in contact with the person they are having a secret relationship with they will run the risk of bringing home their secret telephone. Having an affair is like an addiction to many men and as an addict they cannot go long without their fix of someone telling them how wonderful they are.

It is well documented by the courts that January is the month most couples file for divorce. The Monday of the first full week back at work after New Year is known as 'Divorce Monday.' It would be interesting to know how many of those divorces are based on women finding out their partner had committed adultery.

Remember. . .

- Trust your gut feeling because this is a very powerful, natural instinct.
- Never ignore changes in his behaviour; ask yourself what they might mean.
- Talk about your suspicions but be aware that denial is usually the first port of call.
- Having an affair is like an addiction—men need that validation from the Other-Woman and will often slip up during a break from the normal routine.
- Be aware of his words and whether or not they match his actions.

"When everything seems to be going against you, remember that the airplane takes off against the wind, not with it."

Henry Ford,
American industrialist and founder of the Ford Motor
Company, 1863-1947

Chapter Two

Your Reaction To The Truth

We are now going to discuss how to deal with your emotions and behaviour once you know the truth.

Although evidence may be found which indicates betrayal, some women choose to ignore it for fear of the consequences. To confront him is to acknowledge there may be a serious problem in the relationship. For some women, they feel it is best left unsaid.

This is a common coping mechanism, as many women understandably fear losing their husband, partner, life-long friend and all that goes with it. They often hope that if their partner is having an affair, it will end and no harm will be done.

We make no judgment regarding this decision because we are firm believers that whatever is right for you is to be accepted and supported, without question.

How to deal with your suspicions
You have seen the signs, your suspicions have been alerted, but what do you do now? The first thing you are going to feel is anxiety and with that the need to find out for certain that your partner is cheating on you.

We know how frightening it is to start asking questions,

fearing what you might find out. It's a bit like opening 'Pandora's Box', you don't know what horrors await you, but the temptation is there to know the truth. Don't be scared, only when you know the truth can you begin to move forward. Say to yourself, "I matter, I have to know what I am dealing with."

You are likely to become obsessed with looking for proof of your suspicions. You may turn into someone you don't recognise anymore, because the desire to find out the truth becomes overwhelming. You feel embarrassed at what you are doing, but nothing stops you hunting for the evidence. You will find yourself becoming a hyper-active, super-vigilant, forensic detective!

Common activities women find themselves doing

- Trying to check his telephone when he is not looking.
- Looking for receipts in his pockets and wallet.
- Checking his shirts for makeup marks and his clothes for evidence of sexual activity.
- Accessing his emails.
- Needing to know where he is all the time.
- Tracking his location on smart devices.
- Calling him to ask what he is doing and where he is.
- Watching for anything that is different from his normal behaviour.
- Being hypersensitive regarding how he treats you.

Can you see how a situation like that can start to take over your life?

You may have already voiced your suspicions, only to get

a dismissive response from him. This may leave you feeling frustrated and even more determined to find out what he is up to.

The more you ask him, the more defensive he becomes. Remember, attack is the cheater's first and main line of defence. You try different ways to go about finding the same answer, which is quite simply that he is cheating on you. Is there someone else in his life who threatens your relationship? It becomes a vicious cycle, as the two of you battle in conflict; you trying to discover the truth and him trying to maintain the lie.

At this stage, your health can start to suffer. You may find yourself unable to sleep and eat because you become obsessive about finding out the truth. Your mind is locked into repetitive thoughts and the overwhelming need to know. You are constantly anxious and you struggle to concentrate.

The impact on your daily life is becoming evident. Your friends and family can see that something is troubling you and yet, you don't want to tell them for fear of what they will think. It is easy to become trapped in your own world and inflict more pain on yourself.

Let's remind ourselves that you are still at the stage of not knowing for sure that he is lying to you. Of course, he won't admit it. He may go overboard in trying to prove he is not cheating, in an attempt to put you off the scent! However, as women, we have a sixth sense for these things and until we know the truth we are unable to rest.

When you discover the evidence

You have spent days, weeks, maybe months looking for the evidence that he is having an affair and all of sudden it is staring you in the face. We all find out about our partner's infidelity in different ways and no matter what we think of our partner, we may all have similar feelings of pain and anxiety. You may feel sick to your stomach and the emotions can be so intense they are hard to put into words. The only description that comes close is *excruciating*.

It will feel as though you are walking through treacle for many days. The nights feel long and empty. Often, as you are lying next to him, you feel like attacking him one minute and bursting into tears the next. However, he will start to get edgy because you may be unable to hide your suspicions from him. It might show in your face, your actions and the way you speak to him.

You may feel as if you hate him but do you immediately confront him or do you choose your moment? Alternatively, having found the proof, do you decide to ignore it?

This is a difficult question to answer, because this is where your own personality makes the critical decision about what to do next.

For some women, it is full-blown anger; shouting, screaming, and perhaps physically attacking their partner and/or their belongings. Also, the desire to be as far as possible away from the cheater can be potent for some women.

For other women, it is tears and despair, begging their partner not to leave them, total devastation.

All reactions are consumed by the hurt, which at this point is almost impossible to deal with. You will feel as though you are just about surviving and want more and more evidence to confirm what you already know.

Can you see how quickly all this can spiral out of control?

Even though you have discovered your partner's secret life, there is an increasing desire to know all there is to know. You may be one of those people who have to know the full truth and you can become irrational in your thoughts and actions.

However, there does come a point when you have to stop seeking more truth. You already have the facts that paint the picture and it is now best to stop tormenting yourself looking for more evidence. There simply is no point.

Many women contact us, desperate to know how they should confront their partner once they have found out.

Sasha, a forty-five-year-old Chief Executive Officer with two teenage children from New York said, "I was desperate to confront him when he least expected it. He took me for a fool and thought I didn't know. But he knew something was wrong with me and he pushed and pushed until I exploded and blurted it all out."

We believe the ideal way to confront someone is presented in the scene from the film, *Love Actually*, when Karen (Emma Thompson) confronts Harry (the late Alan Rickman). She tactfully asks him, "What would you do if your husband had bought an expensive necklace at Christmas time, but did not give it to his wife?"

When he slowly begins to realise what she is talking about, she pushes her point strategically, by asking, "Would you wait around to find out if it was just a necklace; or if it was a necklace and sex; or the worst-case scenario, if it was a necklace and love?"

Her final question being, "Would you stay, knowing life would always be a little bit worse, or would you cut and run?"

Of course, Harry understands exactly what she is referring

to and immediately thinks of himself first, saying, "Oh God. I am so in the wrong. A classic fool."

Karen drives her gentle and controlled confrontation home by adding the punch line, "Yes, but you've also made a fool out of me. You've made the life I lead foolish, too."

Very clever, dramatic and deeply hurtful; but in reality, many of us become so incensed and are so hurt that we can't hold it in. The feeling of being made a fool of can be so overwhelming that it takes us over and we lose control over our actions.

Now you know what has been going on, you have to deal with the aftermath. However, let's be clear about the so-called truth. In our experience, you are never going to get the truth, the whole truth and nothing but the truth, no matter how often you ask for it.

If you are convinced he is lying—take action—never ignore your gut instincts.

When your world changes forever

From the moment you discover the truth that your partner is having an affair, your world changes. Even though you were fairly sure you were being betrayed, to actually have it confirmed hits you painfully, like a tonne of bricks.

No matter how much you might try, you cannot escape the process of grief, the loss of what you thought you had, the loss of the person you thought you knew. So many women said the same words to us, "I thought I knew him."

Mandy, a fifty-seven-year-old counsellor with three grown-up children from Ireland said, "I found out that my husband of thirty years had been writing long love poems every day for the woman he was having an affair with. Every morning she woke up to a poem he had sent by email. I was so shocked when I found them as never in all the time I had known him, had he ever written anything romantic for me, yet alone a poem. I really didn't know him at all."

Even if you decide to stay, you will still grieve. You cannot escape the process of grief, you have to surrender to it and accept it. We discuss grief at length in Chapter Twelve: When Staying Together Is Not an Option.

Depending on your personality, you might experience anger or tears first, but be assured, you may feel these emotions with an intensity you have probably never felt before. The emotional energy you expend in these first few minutes can leave you feeling utterly exhausted.

As hard as it is, we strongly recommend that you do not knee-jerk into any decision about the future. It is impossible to think clearly and objectively. What you need to do is seek support as quickly as possible. We understand that for some people this may be too difficult. You may not want friends and family to know, but you need to share your feelings with someone you trust.

Remember, you can always contact us on via our website/email in confidence: hello@keys2life.co.uk.

At a time like this, your dignity can go out of the window. When confronted suddenly by the truth you may display behaviour you never thought yourself capable of. This is the time when you can do and say things you may subsequently regret.

You can find examples of when women in the heat of the moment have taken drastic steps to ensure their partners never cheat again in Chapter Thirteen: Moving On.

Depending on the circumstances you are faced with and

the choices you may or may not have to make to save your relationship, the most important thing is that you do whatever it takes to keep yourself safe and sane.

You must make your day-to-day wellbeing the priority, alongside that of your children, if you have any. You have to make *you* the person whose needs are met at this highly emotional time. If you don't want to involve other members of the family or friends, fine, but you must talk your feelings out. By doing this, you are preventing yourself from falling into the possibility of depression.

There is a valid theory that depression is a result of internalised anger; loss and anger at personal betrayal is certainly at the root of many peoples' depressive episodes. Be aware of this fact and remember it is healthier to release your anger, but only in a safe environment.

Have a pen and piece of paper handy to write down your thoughts and feelings in those moments. Use writing as a way of offloading. You can also use the My Freedom Diary to help you with this process.

Children are very perceptive, especially young children, as much as you may try and keep the situation from them, they are bound to pick up on the vibes. If Daddy has left, they are going to need an explanation.

If your children are aged four years and upwards, they are likely to be more aware than you think. You need to tell them something, for to leave them without any form of explanation could increase their anxiety, not lessen it.

Children need to know a reason as to why you are upset, why Daddy has left or why Mummy and Daddy are not happy.

When you don't say anything, they will be left to make

up their own story and this inevitably involves fear and abandonment. You are struggling to deal with your own feelings and the fallout of knowing the truth. As hard as it is to find the strength of mind to address the emotions of your children, you really do need to do this.

If your children are close to friends and family or grandparents, ask for their help in conveying love and care towards your children at this very turbulent time. There is more information about how to support your children in Chapter Eight: His Other People *Script*.

When tears come first, anger will not be far behind and when you feel this anger you are going to respond in one of two ways. You will deal with it by either 'acting in' or 'acting out.'

Acting in means you will turn the pain against yourself.

Acting out means you will try to temporarily dull the emotional pain with some kind of vengeful behaviour.

Be careful, you must keep yourself safe, particularly if you are in a physically abusive relationship. Do not confront your partner with your suspicions without being in a place of safety and with the right support.

Acting in

Depending on your personality, you will either feel comfortable expressing anger or not. Some women go to great lengths to deny and repress their anger because they fear that people will perceive them to be unstable or mad. Their cheating partner may have given this impression to many people already.

The anger has to go somewhere and if you are not the type of person to outwardly express it, then the anger is going to stay inside and it may manifest itself in several ways.

You may:
- Have trouble eating and sleeping.
- Become depressed.
- Feel high anxiety.
- Become more irritable.
- Start drinking too much.
- Develop physical symptoms that you have never had before, such as an upset stomach.
- Find yourself comfort eating.
- Not be able get control of your thoughts.
- Keep going over and over the lies, trying to find a reason for the cause of the betrayal.

By acting in the ways described above and by not venting your anger safely, you are punishing yourself. You may want to avoid confrontation with your partner by downplaying your pain and anger, but the price is far too high on you.

By acting in and internalising your anger, you are on the rocky road to losing your identity.

Acting out
If you are the type of person to act out your anger you may be inclined to display destructive behaviour.

Examples of what a person can do when they are not in control of their anger are below.

You may:
- Go to his place of work and cause a scene.
- Start divorce proceedings immediately.
- Attempt to make contact with his Other-Woman.

- Call everyone you know and tell them what he has done.
- Destroy or damage things that are important to him, such as scratching his car or cutting up his clothes.
- Excessive revenge spending.
- Excessive use of alcohol.
- Revenge sex with someone your partner knows.

In the moment you may feel joyful retribution and revenge. For some people, those feelings may persist, for others a sense of guilt and remorse can subsequently take hold. You may find yourself asking the question, *"How could I do what I have done?"* The response from your partner, which may be anger, might lead you to feel more despair.

The need for revenge stems from the pain you are suffering, which can consume you. Vengeful acts can end very badly and may have the opposite effect to what you wanted; sometimes pushing him closer to the Other-Woman. This can be because your partner feels responsible for your actions and wants to protect the Other-Woman. It can also justify all the things he has been telling her about you.

Miriam, a fifty-year-old mother of three children from London, told us how she messaged all the contacts in her husband's mobile phone, including his work colleagues; wrote the word 'slag' on the Other-Woman's car; and packed up all his clothes and threw them in the garden of the Other-Woman.

This only gave her husband the justification to continue his affair because she was 'insane and uncontrollable'.

She said, "I felt as though I had lost my moral high ground and regretted it, especially when he filed for divorce on the grounds of unreasonable behaviour and cited what I had done."

However, it is natural to want revenge. We know that for some women the feelings of needing to take revenge can be so consuming that they take control of rational thoughts. We know that many acts of revenge are impulsive, but we strongly recommend that you refer to the My Freedom Diary and write out your feelings and thoughts on paper first. This will help to prevent you from doing something you may regret in the future. Also, talk to someone you trust and tell them how you feel. Let it out and release it.

Money is often used as both a weapon of revenge and a control when a relationship breaks down. Some men who are the major breadwinners in the family try to control their partner by cutting off their finances.

Hannah, a thirty-one-year-old full-time mother from Seattle, told us how her husband cut off her access to their joint bank account and she didn't even have the money to buy petrol to get their young son to school. He booked a holiday to Disneyland for himself and their four-year-old son leaving her alone at home with no money for food.

She said, "He wanted to see me beg and realise how much I needed him. He thought he could control me by leaving me penniless."

Revenge spending—wanting to literally 'make him pay'—is a way some women deal with their hurt and anger. There have been several high-profile examples of revenge spending.

In England, it was claimed in 2015 by Liam Gallagher of *Oasis* fame that his ex-wife Nicole Appleton had indulged in revenge spending when she found out he had fathered a child with an American journalist.

In America, the wife of Yankee Ball player, Alex Rodriguez

ran up a debt of US$100,000 when she discovered his affair with Madonna.

Banks are aware of the risk of revenge spending between separating couples and can take legal action that for many women results in them feeling like a victim for a second time.

Gabby, a fifty-four-year-old University lecturer from Norfolk, is now divorced, but had been married for twenty years. She told us how she went to pay for her supermarket groceries and her bankcards were rejected. When she rang the bank, she was told that because she was going through divorce proceedings and was a second cardholder on her husband's account, she had become a 'risk' and the bank had stopped her cards.

"I felt totally humiliated and so angry. My husband had been buying designer shoes, jewellery and handbags for the Other-Woman, but I couldn't pay for my groceries. I didn't have the affair but once again I was left feeling like the victim."

If you are set on revenge, be wise and subtle about it.

Philippa, a thirty-five-year-old lawyer from Nottingham had been married for ten years and has a six-year-old son. She told us she took great gratification from carefully and methodically unpicking a few odd stitches from each of her husband's suit trousers and shirts.

During the course of a year, he began complaining that his trousers had split at the most inappropriate times and the buttons of his shirts kept flying off! He thought it was merely a run of bad luck and didn't associate it with her. She smiled to herself each time and wished she had been a fly on the wall to see his embarrassment.

There are more positive ways to constructively deal with

your anger. For example, you could write him a letter; beat the pillow; or put a picture of your partner on an empty chair and scream and shout at it all you like. You could go to the gym and workout all your anger.

Christine, a fifty-year-old doctor from Liverpool, said that she joined a kick boxing class and imagined the punch bag was her husband's head!

She said, "My coach told me that I didn't hit as hard once I was divorced!"

Remember. . .

- The most important thing is that you do whatever it takes to keep yourself safe and sane.
- It is better for your health to express your anger appropriately—not by 'acting in' or 'acting out.'
- Before you do something like revenge spending, consider the longer-term implications of the actions you are taking out of a place of anger.
- Ask for help from friends and family to support you and, if you have any, your children, cope with the major changes and turbulence impacting your family home.
- Find a distraction in things that will give you purpose, for example focus on your career or family.

"I did not have sexual relations with that woman."

William Jefferson 'Bill' Clinton
American politician, forty-second President of the USA
between 1993 and 2001

Chapter Three

His Denial Script

We are going to guide you through the *script* he uses when he has been found out; deny, deny and deny. We look at his excuses and how you can respond to and manage them. The reason he will deny everything is to make out that you are the one who has got it wrong; so he can hide behind his denial and continue the relationships, both with you and the Other-Woman.

Not only do most men have a *script* embedded in their brains for when they are cheating, but also for when they have been found out. They usually come up with similar reasons for their infidelity, often focusing the blame entirely on their partner. One man blamed his wife's "grovelling loveliness." Some men will say anything to excuse their behaviour!

Their first reaction is always to deny. In Chapter Five: His Own *Script*—we deal with the words of an adulterous male and what he tells himself.

Men may take some responsibility while they think they have you on side, but once you start to challenge them or they are not getting their own way, they can come up with very similar excuses.

Most cheating men are skilled in the act of rewriting history.

They change and twist the circumstances of events to give themselves an excuse as to why they had an affair.

Sylvia, a forty-three-year-old caterer from Chester and a mother of three children, had lived with her husband for twenty years before they decided to marry. She was reluctant to marry him because he had cheated on her previously, for more than six years, with a work colleague.

Finally, she thought she could trust him and believed he would never hurt her again. Sadly, two years after getting married she discovered he was cheating on her again.

When she challenged her partner and asked why he wanted to marry her in the first place, he said, "I thought I would never cheat on you again, but you made me cheat because you hadn't forgiven me for the first time."

She was totally shocked and said, "I wrote in my wedding speech that I had forgiven him and moved on. The past was gone and it was only the future that mattered. I said it in front of all our family and friends and I meant it. Yet he made it his excuse to say I hadn't forgiven him, he said my wedding speech had put pressure on him to be someone he wasn't."

Alicia, a thirty-nine-year-old estate agent from Wales, said, "I realised it didn't matter what I did or what I said, it was always turned around to be my fault. It was my fault that my husband had to keep seeing his Other-Woman. My fault he had to leave. It took me leaving the marriage to realise that everything wasn't my fault, it was his!"

If you have discovered that your partner is having an affair, how many excuses from the list below have you heard? We have divided these into three categories.

Excuses

One set of excuses: your fault

- You were not there when I needed you to listen to me.
- You spend more time talking to your friends than me.
- You only have time for the children, leaving me feeling frozen out.
- You put everyone else before me.
- You are obsessed with your job.
- You spend too much money.
- You drink too much.
- You don't look after yourself and you are a mess.
- You don't let me anywhere near you.
- You don't show me affection.
- We never have sex.
- You don't understand me.
- You told me it was over between us.
- It is all in your head.

Another set of excuses: his justification

- I didn't plan it, it just happened.
- I thought you didn't love me.
- It was a fantasy it wasn't real. It was just a bit of fun and excitement.
- Everyone does it.
- I was drunk.
- It only happened once.
- I felt guilty all the time, as I was really thinking about you.

- I have learned my lesson and I will never do it again.
- I have learned my lesson and I have changed.
- A man has needs.
- I was stupid and wasn't thinking straight.
- It is in my genes and there is nothing I can do about it!

More excuses: it's not what it seems

- I love *you*.
- I don't want to lose you.
- She is just a friend.
- She means nothing to me.
- I don't know anything about her, really.
- I don't even know where she lives.
- It is not what it looks like.

Let's talk about these lines of his *script*; what they really mean and how you can deal with them. We are guessing you have heard quite a few of them before?

Your fault

Here's a quote from a husband who said to his wife, when she had caught him out, *"Why do you have to be so fucking clever?"*

In other words, "Why can't you let me carry on with my affair? Instead of proving that I am continually lying to you?"

This is most certainly not your fault. No matter how bad your relationship problems are, even if both of you are not perfect, you did not make a decision to go outside the partnership and have an affair or push him to do it either. He is one hundred percent to blame. If he didn't talk to you before he cheated, how were you to know anything was wrong in your relationship?

If he fires all your faults at you as justification for him cheating, ask him calmly, "So why tell me now? Why didn't you tell me before you cheated on me?"

Without a doubt, in stating it is your fault, he will have used several of the excuses we listed.

It may be that you are busy making a safe and secure future for your family, giving most of your time to nurturing your children or looking after your family and friends. This is life and these relationships mould what we are.

Men will always try and push the blame onto someone else. While you have been a good partner, mother, housekeeper, career woman, he now blames you for not giving him all your time. Chances are that you haven't had any time to think about yourself, let alone him.

Men start to blame women when we are at one of the lowest points in our life; at the very moment when we have discovered his affair. At that point, we can't think straight. For example, how often do you start a sentence and then can't remember what you were talking about? You are in such emotional turmoil you can hardly function.

Many of you may be trying to hide his affair from your children, family and friends for fear of being judged, embarrassed and ashamed. Many women compare it to feeling like a clown, living in a parallel universe, not being connected to real life—but having to smile on the outside while crippled with pain on the inside.

When men blame women in this way, it often forces us to believe what they are saying and to believe we are to blame. If he keeps telling you that you are to blame, keep reading the section on blame, to reassure yourself that it is not your fault.

Rosie, a sixty-one-year-old retired civil servant from Hampshire, told us how she felt as though she had the *Sword of Damocles* hanging over her head by a fine hair, ready to stab her every time she said or did the wrong thing.

Her husband of thirty years had an affair with a much younger woman. He kept telling her it was finished, but every time she challenged or questioned him he would use it as an excuse to go back to the Other-Woman.

He kept telling her, "It is your fault, you left me no option but to go back. You pushed me away, even though it was finished you sent me spiralling back."

The really sad thing is that despite Rosie being an extremely intelligent and rational woman, she started to question herself and think maybe it was actually her fault. Her husband manipulated her mind by using her vulnerability as an excuse for his appalling treatment of her.

His justification

Your partner may have told you, "It's just what us men do."

In fact, we have heard the families of men who have betrayed their partners saying things like, "Well, it is how French/Italian/Greek men are."

There is no justification.

Forty-four-year-old Pietra, a policewoman with no children from Antigua, said her husband told her, "It was just a bit of fun and excitement, which got out of hand." His Other-Woman then used exactly the same words. This totally floored her and sent her into a deep spiral of increasing poor self-esteem.

She said, "How could he belittle my marriage so flippantly and make me feel so worthless and insignificant?"

Other excuses frequently used by unfaithful men are "I was drunk" or "It only happened once."

See these excuses for what they really are; being drunk is not an excuse; if he was that drunk he probably wouldn't have been able to have sex! It only happened once; men use this as if it makes it better. It doesn't make any difference—once, twice, a hundred times, it is still betrayal. It happened and the images will be there, in your head, for a long time.

It's not what it seems

Eman, a thirty-six-year-old divorced artist from Egypt, had actually seen her husband on several occasions with the Other-Woman. He had told her she was imagining it and she was mentally ill. With low and poor self-esteem, combined with a lack of confidence, she started to doubt her own sanity.

She said, "I became so confused about everything and couldn't focus or get clarity in my mind. A friend told me to make notes, so I started to write everything in my diary, events, days, times when my husband was working late or away, his mood, anything really. I also wrote how I was feeling. Once I started to correlate everything and could see it clearly in black and white, I knew he was lying and cruelly tormenting me by saying I was imagining it all.

"Now, looking back, my diary was my saving grace because my mind was so muddled, I would never have remembered times and dates etc. I lived in a permanent fog, with such poor self-esteem for nearly a year. I am so glad I wrote it all down, because not only did it give me the evidence I needed to confront my husband, it also helps me now, to see how far I have come on days when I doubt myself.

"I did give my husband a second chance, but he continued his affair, which for me was the final straw. I survived betrayal and it made me know what is right for me. I am now happy and have a clear head. My ex-husband is still with that Other-Woman and I have heard he is unhappy. I don't know how she stayed with him, knowing what he is capable of, but that is their life now, it certainly isn't mine."

Without doubt one of the cruellest actions a cheating partner can do is to carry on with the affair while pretending it is finished. The psychological nightmare women find themselves experiencing when this happens can be so severe it can lead to PTSD.

Symptoms of PTSD include: difficulty controlling your emotions; periods of losing concentration; obsessive thought and flashbacks; nightmares; cutting yourself off from friends and family; and/or partaking in destructive or risky behaviour, such as self-harm and suicidal thoughts.

One of the primary symptoms of PTSD is losing trust in people and is it any wonder that you would have a lack of trust, given the situation you have just found yourself in? Of course, not all women will suffer with PTSD but if you relate to any of the symptoms we have mentioned, then please do not hesitate to contact your doctor and seek medical support.

Some men can be so convincing when lying to your face, that even when you have concrete evidence, somehow you can have doubts in your head and start to question your own state of mind. This is because you cannot believe this person who you loved so much could treat you so badly.

It is easy to feel completely crushed by this behaviour and to remain strong and focused is almost impossible. This is the time to really accept the person for who they truly are and not who you thought they were.

Lisa, a forty-year-old mother of three from St Albans, told us how she felt when her husband told her his Other-Woman was pregnant. When she started to shake and feel as though her world had collapsed, he went on to tell her that it was not what it seemed.

"She was desperate for a baby so I wanted to help her. I didn't have sex with her, I was just a donor," he claimed.

He explained to her how he did it and though she actually had a science background and knew what he was describing was impossible, she started to doubt her own knowledge and experience.

We imagine as you are reading these examples you are probably wondering why these women took ownership of their partners' affairs? And blamed the affairs on themselves? It is obvious to those people on the outside, but when you are the one on the receiving end you can't see what he is telling you for what it really is—an outright lie, an excuse and a justification for his appalling behaviour.

Many men will also say, "Oh she is just a friend, I have known her for years." Well, if this is true, why have you never met this good friend? It is surprising how many men use this as an excuse for a secret friendship.

When you ask to meet her, you will probably get a response such as, "Oh, she is really busy, I don't know how to contact her" or "I don't know where she lives." In essence, he will come up with every excuse in the book as to why you should not meet with her.

As with all affairs, this is a part that is really hard to get into perspective; it is the nagging thought that someone knows your partner that well, yet you know nothing about her. If she is the clichéd 'shoulder to cry on' what has he said to need that shoulder? We torment ourselves wondering what he has told her about our private life.

You are probably asking yourself, w*hat right does he have to talk to someone about me?*

You hate the fact that someone out there is walking about knowing your private feelings and yet, you may know nothing about them, or even what they look like. You could sit next to that woman on a train and not know who she is, yet she may know everything about you. We strongly recommend that you seek professional help, if possible, from a relationship counsellor.

Remember. . .

- It is most certainly not your fault.
- Never take responsibility for his actions.
- Know the symptoms of PTSD and do not hesitate to seek medical help if they begin to apply to you.
- Seek counselling / therapy to move beyond the worries of what the Other-Woman knows about you and your life.
- Try not to doubt yourself, your experiences, your knowledge, what you know to be true.

"It's not what happens to you, it's what you do about it that makes the difference."

Wilson Mitchell
American novelist and physicist, 1914-1973

Chapter Four

Your Response

At this point we can focus on helping you deal with how you react to the discovery of an affair by acknowledging your feelings and making sense of the lies. The My Freedom Diary will also really help you with your response by giving you clarity and focus.

Being betrayed annihilates who you are and the world you once knew. We can only describe it as a bullet that comes out of the blue. It blows a hole in your heart and ricochets everywhere; hurting the world around you and the people closest to you. It is a bullet that is totally out of your control.

Even though you had your suspicions, one of the first emotions might be utter shock. This, mixed with immense pain and anger, fear and confusion, makes any initial communication with him very difficult to deal with.

You will want to know everything. Who? When? Where? How long? You will want to know what he feels about her, but this is such a loaded question that you may be tempted not to ask. However, in our opinion it needs to be asked sooner, rather than later. Why? Because you need to know if your relationship has a chance of being saved or not—and you need to know this as soon as possible. Knowing what he feels for this Other-Woman is going to give you some clarity as to the options that now confront you.

Acknowledge how you are feeling

Your feelings will be all over the place. Your mind will be in absolute turmoil. Finding out the truth may have left you feeling sick, unable to eat or sleep, worried and fearful for the future. If you have children, they will be of huge concern to you, knowing your relationship may be at an end.

After finding out about the affair many women told us that they have felt and thought several of the following responses:

- I thought I knew him.
- I thought he would never do this to me.
- I don't know what is real and what is not anymore.
- I don't know the man I see.
- My life and dreams have been blown out of the water.
- I don't know who I am anymore.
- I want to punish him.

However, remember that many men find it hard to talk about their feelings. Although women often feel the need to talk, we have to accept that most men react in a different way to us.

Women often also ask themselves the following questions in the aftermath of the discovery:

- Am I to blame?
- Is it my fault?
- Could I have done more to prevent this from happening?

Pay serious attention to these three questions because depending on your answers you could be heading down a road you definitely want to avoid. This path will only cause you more pain and heartache.

These questions are about wrongly taking on the responsibility for your partner's affair. You are looking for evidence to suggest that you have given him the reasons to have this relationship with another woman.

It is very important—when reflecting on your relationship and the part you played in it—that you remember it was his choice to have an affair. His choice. You didn't make him do anything, despite his possible protestations to the contrary.

Blaming you is a cowardly and cruel response that deflects the responsibility for his actions away from him and on to you. Do not be fooled by this and do not accept responsibility for his actions.

Initially, you may be in shock, which inhibits your brain to see things clearly. Some of us can barely function and get through the day. You may well accept you are to blame and for this reason, you may well find yourself accepting accusations that are in no way factual. This is a really important point to understand.

Think about the question, *Could I have done more to prevent the affair from happening?*

Once again, the focus is on you and not on you both. He had equal responsibility to talk about his desires and feelings as much as you. If he didn't do that, how could you know that he might not be happy?

Maybe you noticed that things weren't so good between you and maybe you had tried to talk to him about it, only to be met with a dismissive and defensive attitude. This is not your fault either, but rather his, through his refusal to acknowledge your need to talk about your desires and feelings. However, if he has aired his feelings and you chose to ignore him, then you do have to take responsibility for that action.

Of course, it still does not mean you made him have an affair; it remains his choice. However, remember that many men find it hard to talk about their feelings, leaving their partner even more frustrated.

How to make sense of the lies

The person who once was your friend has now become your enemy and the loss you feel in that situation is so huge, you may find yourself wanting to believe the lies.

You now know your partner has been having an affair. If you have been seeking the truth, you have finally got your answer. You are feeling utterly betrayed and the lies, which have been such a part of his guilt and denial, are staring you hard in the face. Now what do you do? A man who puts you through months or even years of torment has an enormous capacity to lie.

You may try to rationalise his lying. The reason you do this is because you want to find a way of forgiving him, so your relationship can survive. You can look for good reasons to justify his lying and this nearly almost always accompanies his 'good reasons' for why he has had an affair.

For example, he may tell you that he never wanted to have an affair and he never wanted to hurt you. Buying into the phrase, 'never wanted to hurt you' could encourage you to hang on to the belief that he loves you. You make an excuse for him, which implies that his actions were not under his control. By doing this, you are giving him an excuse not to take full responsibility for his choice and actions. You are more likely to do this when you want your relationship to survive.

By refusing to accept the reality, you are actually lying to yourself. By rationalising his lies, you are deluding yourself into a false sense of comfort.

Moira, a sixty-four-year-old from Aberdeen with three grandchildren, wrote to us and said, "My husband totally blind-sided me with lie after lie. He told me I was crazy and I started to believe it."

Remember one lie can make you question a thousand truths. Be true to yourself. We mean be completely honest with what you feel, value and desire. Being true to yourself also means that you don't live by someone else's standards and rules. It is not about pleasing other people.

This does not mean that you are inconsiderate or disrespectful of other people, it means that you will not let other people define you or make decisions for you that you should be making for yourself.

How to deal with the changes in your life

An affair changes your life forever; a change you did not want or expect. The decision to stay or go may be yours, but equally many of you may not have had that choice if your partner has left to be with another person.

Is it possible that this unwanted change in your life could bring about new possibilities? Some you never thought about before the pain of betrayal in your relationship?

The way you think about this change will hugely impact

the way you feel. Your thoughts are either going to empower you to move forward or prevent you from becoming positively independent.

The pain of anger, loss, fear and shame can be an excellent motivator in helping you to want to move forward into a place where you start to leave the bad feelings behind. By doing this you are taking responsibility for your own life and probably those who are dependent on you, such as your children.

These emotions are your responses to being let down and cheated on—the feeling that your partner has taken control of your life. He can only do this if you allow him to. He cannot control your identity unless you let him.

For many years your identity has been as a part of a couple and suddenly you find yourself alone. This requires a huge adjustment. It is like finding your feet again as an individual. And be warned, this feeling can continue to exist, even if you decide to stay. This is especially the case if he doesn't allow you to talk freely about his affair.

You have got to focus on valuing yourself; think about your self-worth and your self-respect and how you deserve to be loved and appreciated. Think about all that you do and the various roles you play in your life. Now, think about your partner. Have you valued each other equally? Have you felt truly loved and understood in your relationship?

You need to be realistic in your assessment because this will help you lessen the pain and move forward. Change is happening whether you like it or not. Somehow you have to turn the resentment into a motivating factor, which drives you towards making your life the best it can be, with the circumstances you have been given.

Setting small goals for yourself can really help. In the initial phase, you might not be able to do this, but as time goes on it is helpful to think about how you would like your life to be in the future.

Feel, manage and repair the pain

Our primary objective when we feel pain is to do whatever it takes to get rid of it as quickly as possible. You cannot avoid the pain of betrayal, but you do have the ability to control it. There is a big difference between feeling emotional pain and continuing to suffer.

Pain as a positive motivator for change

When you use the pain in the right way, it can be a motivating factor towards positive change. A change that empowers you, so the act of betrayal becomes a freeing experience.

Repairing the scars of pain

When you have discovered your partner's infidelity and you are in deep pain it is telling you that something is really, really, wrong. That might be stating the obvious, however, if you don't listen to what your emotions are telling you, then inevitably the healing process is going to take much longer and may lead to more confusion about how to deal with your partner and what happens next.

Having discovered the affair, the most important thing for you to work out is, how are you going to heal from it? Healing is not about denial and it is not about suppressing your true feelings. Neither can he be allowed to carry on as if the affair never happened.

Healing from his affair is in your control. You may not be able to escape the emotional pain, but you can make a decision not to continue the suffering.

For many women, the crippling physical pain they feel after being betrayed stems from the feeling of the 'love' they have for their partner. How many times have we heard a woman who has been badly treated say, "But I love him!"

It is important to remind ourselves of what love means. Most definitions of love agree that it is, *'An intense feeling of romantic attachment based on an attraction felt by one person for another; intense liking and concern for another person, typically combined with sexual passion.'*

Notice the words 'intense liking and concern.' You need to look beyond the affair and your feelings of love and ask yourself, *I may think I love him, but do I like him?*

During our research for The MAN*Script*, we asked numerous London taxi drivers questions about their relationships. Taxi drivers form a captive audience, often enjoy a good discussion and they can't back away! We weren't left on the side of the road for prying, but there were certainly quite a few red necks at the front of the cab!

We asked one man, "Would you cheat or have you cheated on your wife?"

He immediately said, "No, I would never do that because I have too much respect for her. She is my best friend."

Think carefully about the following questions:
- Do I like the fact that my partner didn't show concern for me?
- Do I like the fact that my partner didn't show me respect?

- Do I like the fact that he is a liar?
- Do I like the fact that he has deliberately hurt me without any thought for me?
- Do I like the fact that he is a cheat?
- Do I like the fact that he is devious?
- Do I like the character of the partner I thought I once knew?
- Would I like him as a friend?

We do not ask you the question, "Do you love him?"

You may think you love him, but given what he has done, do you like him? If you had the option of having him as a close friend of yours, would you have him?

This pain that you are feeling is about someone who has totally disrespected you as a person, ignored all the qualities that you have and dismissed all the years of love, care and attention. Are you going to let him now destroy the rest of your life and you with it?

Leanne, a thirty-seven-year-old Head of Communications for a television network from Los Angeles, told us, "I don't know who I am anymore. I have gone from a happy, trusting person to an angry, nervous wreck. The pain is crippling me."

Is he such a wonderful person given what you now know with all the newly revealed character traits? Would you rather have him back in your life only to use and abuse you again? Or are you going to dig deep and find the strength to turn your back on the person who has let you down and disappointed you so badly?

You must focus on your self-care and first of all, nourish your body with good healthy food; a little is better than none at all. Try not to fall into the trap of not eating—or bingeing on unhealthy foods—because you are so distraught. Take some exercise; a short walk is better than sitting on the sofa hiding from the world.

Keep telling yourself:
- I matter, I matter, I matter! (Repeat, repeat and repeat.)
- I am worthy of respect and love.
- I refuse to let my partner damage my self-worth and self-esteem.
- I am strong.
- I am resilient.

Finally, do not be afraid or embarrassed to seek the company of people who are going to help you through this very difficult time. We can't stress enough that it is essential you do this. The temptation to hide away can be great but our advice is to do the opposite.

As hard as we know this can be at times, you are not alone and once you are brave enough to talk out your thoughts, you may be surprised at how many other people have been through a similar experience.

We know it is easy to say but putting it into practice can be difficult. Start by inviting a trusted friend to come over to see you, then you can step out for lunch, or for a walk, or to a café. Try to attend an event or do something alone to help you feel empowered.

Don't be afraid to do things you enjoy to try to make yourself feel better.

It is also essential that you understand where the pain, inflicted by your partner, stems from. Depending on your personality, it might come from any of the following feelings:

- Rejection.
- Disrespect.
- Disregard.
- Unloved.
- Being made a fool of.
- Your feelings being dismissed.
- No longer being number one in their life.

Self-inflicted pain

The pain caused by betrayal can actually make us believe that all of the above is who we are. By colluding with those beliefs, we end up increasing the pain within ourselves. We understand that this is a really hard place, not only to find yourself in, but to be able to repair yourself from. This can be difficult to achieve alone and it is where therapy can be so helpful. You are also very welcome to contact us at hello@keys2life.co.uk

If you decide to stay in a relationship, the lack of trust is one of the key issues to recover from. The pain caused by a lack of trust gives rise to the feelings of immense fear, anxiety, agitation, anger, paranoia, loss of appetite and depression. This is why your partner has to be one hundred percent transparent. Clarity is the most important part of the healing process, after an affair.

If the man is not prepared to do this or to have the patience and empathy to understand your feelings, you have an important choice to make.

If you decide to stay in a relationship like this, then you become the perpetrator of your own pain by staying with a man who isn't prepared (or hasn't the ability) to help you regain your trust in him. In this case, the responsibility for any continuing pain lies with you.

You may find yourself in this position if you have decided to stay in the relationship. If so, it is the time to ask yourself, why? Is the need for stability at the core of your decision? Is it your concern for the children; your financial situation; or something else?

Staying in a painful situation can lead to a feeling of losing control. This can result in ill health and depression. When you are depressed, it is much harder to have the strength to balance your self-esteem to reduce the pain.

What makes you vulnerable to staying in pain?
Some of the characteristics that can contribute to you staying in a state of near constant pain are as follows:

- Personality.
- Family traits and experiences.
- Characteristic traits such as a fear of being alone.
- Previous relationship experiences.
- Your tendency to think on the positive or negative side.
- Insecure childhood experiences.
- Lack of confidence.
- Medical issues.
- Financial worries.
- Responsibility for children.

- Responsibility for other people, such as elderly parents.
- Fear of ending a relationship because of the potential consequences.

Ask yourself the questions:
- Am I prepared to stay in this relationship, even though I do not trust my partner, and he will not help me heal, but causes me to feel pain on a daily basis?
- I will suffer this pain because my greater need is. . .?

Fill in the gap in the latter question for yourself. Now you have done that, you have identified what your payoff is for the pain you have sustained. However, there are ways to reduce that pain. For some women this is their children, for others it is fear of financial insecurity, and for others it is a feeling of 'I must not fail.'

Repair the pain
The pain is telling you that something needs to change. Betrayal and all that comes with it can lead to the worse emotional pain you have ever felt. It can challenge every part of you and who you are.

Whatever the circumstances, or the people involved, it is time to stop permitting them to affect your identity, self-esteem, confidence and ability to sustain yourself in daily life. Only you can decide when you are ready to take action. Only you can decide when you have had enough and are prepared to fight back. Fighting back means having respect for yourself and refusing to allow anyone else to take that from you.

Ask yourself the following questions:
- What would it feel like to be free of suspicion and pain?
- What would have to happen to achieve this?
- What action can I take that will help me move towards a place where I feel empowered and in control?
- What is the worst that can happen from the situation I am in?
- How would I cope if the (above question) worst happened?
- What strategies can I put in place now to minimise the impact, should the worst happen?

We all have the potential to get trapped by our life experiences. To be free and connected you need to invest in your own personal happiness, which means being in touch with your needs and desires. If you can overcome your own need to stay attached to something that is no longer beneficial to you and is in fact causing you harm, then you can see the pain as an opportunity to expand your life in a positive way, rather than restrict it.

Whether you are reconciling your relationship, or it is finished, you cannot escape the pain and therefore, you really need to make yourself the priority. Making yourself the priority means you refuse to be on the receiving end of behaviour that disrespects your feelings. Once you are able to do this, you will start to become stronger and the pain will lessen.

Remember. . .
- Healing from his affair is in your control.
- No one can control your identity unless you let them.
- What is the worst that could happen? Identify this fear as it will help you assess your options.
- What is making you susceptible to staying in this state of pain long-term? Consider previous relationships, your childhood experiences, your personality and character traits—are they contributing to this feeling of extreme pain?
- Look in the mirror every morning and tell yourself out loud: 'I matter, I matter, I matter.'

"A lie gets halfway around the world before the truth has a chance its get its pants on!"

Sir Winston Churchill,
British politician and 1953 Nobel Prize winner for literature,
1874-1965

Chapter Five

His Own Script

We know (and understand) that some of you will have skipped straight to this part of The MAN*Script*. Here we share with you the experiences, anecdotes and comments that men have shared with us during our research for this book. They share their experiences of cheating on their partners and reveal the *script* they tell/have told themselves.

It includes:
- No one will find out.
- She will be grateful, because I won't be asking her for sex.
- What she doesn't know can't hurt her.
- I won't get caught.
- It is just a physical thing.
- I am going through a mid-life crisis.

Men's interpretations of their *scripts* in their own words

During the research for writing this book, we spoke with men who had cheated on their partners; some had had numerous affairs. This conversation in itself was very challenging because their built-in denial *script* makes it almost impossible for them to open the door to their inner thoughts and processes. They struggle through the truth, perhaps only revealing aspects of it after a long period of time and usually, only when they really are caught with nowhere else to go.

The following are anecdotes and comments from the men we spoke to who shared their experience in their own words. Our comments are in brackets. At the end of each account we give our thoughts about their *scripts* and then summarise the commonalities between them all. This first story is a classic case of a man who uses justification to defend himself.

Alan's story (and *script*)

Alan is a fifty-five-year-old engineer living in Berkshire, married for twenty-five years, with two children.

"I never set out to hurt my wife or have an affair *(the classic; I didn't plan it, it just happened defence)*. It wasn't about sex, but sex became part of it at a later stage.

"When I first met her I thought she was nice. Over time we exchanged emails and I found she had a great sense of humour, this soon moved to text messages, which became more and more funny. We just laughed. I didn't actually have face-to-face contact with her for several months after I first met her because we met through work and she worked at another company office quite some distance away.

"By sheer coincidence, I ended up having to visit the office where she worked and on that first occasion we had a quick drink after work *(was it really sheer coincidence?)* I then had to visit her office on more occasions. This wasn't contrived; it was just the way my work sent me.

"The next time I was at her office, we went out for a longer drink and something to eat. It was all very innocent at that stage (*they may not have had sex, but would his wife have seen it as innocent, when he had been having flirtatious text conversations with her?*) but it was obvious we both liked each other and got on.

"At that time, there were a number of stresses in my marriage and there had been for two or three years. In simple terms, things were not always very good at home and I suppose I was unhappy.

"For months, I and this other person exchanged text messages and would also talk on the telephone. The next time I was at her office we went out for a meal after work and we both got very drunk. We didn't realise what the time was and when she tried to get a cab to take her home, none were available. I offered for her to stay in my hotel room, on the understanding I would be a perfect gentleman, which I was. Nothing happened, we both simply fell asleep.

"She wasn't married and didn't have children, but she was in a relationship with a boyfriend of several years.

"After that night, I think we both realised that something more could happen between us. We skirted around the issue for weeks, until eventually we agreed to set a boundary line in respect of our relationship that neither of us was going to cross. (*If he had to set boundaries in a 'friendship' then he was already betraying his partner*).

"I saw her on another occasion and we did abide by the rules we had set. I think it was the next time though, when we got drunk together again and she stayed in my hotel room that we ended up crossing the boundary line.

"The next day, for both of us, there was the mixed emotion

of surprise, guilt, excitement and regret. We both knew what we had done was madness. However, as time went on, having taken that first step, we met every time I was at her office and our relationship became just fun and excitement and something we both looked forward to. By then it was a very sexual relationship.

"We lived in a cosy, secret little world that allowed us both to escape from the other pressures of our lives. In the time we had together, we probably enjoyed our secret little world on no more than six occasions in a period of a year or so. That does not excuse what we did, of course.

"In the end, my wife began to suspect that something was not right and she took steps to prove her suspicions. Clearly, I did something or acted in a way that caused those suspicions to be raised in the first place.

"When the affair was discovered, my immediate thoughts were to protect the Other-Woman, not my wife. Why was that I'm sure you ask? I think and I'm trying to be totally honest here, it was because there had been issues with my wife; over a period of time I thought I had tried really hard to support her and, in my view, at that time, she had thrown that support back in my face. She had also done some things, which in my view amounted to her not supporting me.

"I know women view adultery or cheating on them as the ultimate betrayal, but for men, well certainly for me, you can betray someone in other ways too. It sounds like I am blaming my wife and at the time of these events, I think I probably did.

"With hindsight and reflection, nothing my wife did justified my actions. After a while when things had moved on, I realised how cruel my initial reaction had been and how

I had completely devastated and destroyed my wife through what I had done.

"I wanted to protect my Other-Woman because in my view she had only ever been good to me. She had been my friend and given me moments of happiness away from the other pressures in my life. She had actually done me good and helped me deal with those other pressures. That was how I felt at the time.

"There was also another element to this. I know any woman reading this won't agree, but my Other-Woman was actually a really nice person. In all other ways she was good, kind, caring, thoughtful and cared about other people. If my wife had met her, in other circumstances, I think she would probably think the same.

"When our affair began, the Other-Woman was really worried about my children and the risk of what being found out might do to my family. She was adamant that what we were doing had to be kept completely secret to protect everyone else from harm." *(If she was so concerned about his kids, she would never have slept with a married man in the first place!)*

"Equally, in all other aspects I think I am a good and honest person too. If I saw some money lying on the pavement I would take it to a police station. I'm not a deceitful or dishonest person in any other part of my life, in fact, quite the opposite. It is only in this one respect that I have been weak, dishonest and untruthful.

"Speaking as a man, I think I deal with things in black and white and separate aspects of my life into compartments. As I said, I never set out to hurt my wife, damage my home life or hurt my children. So long as the two aspects of my life were kept apart, in my mind, even though I knew what I was doing was wrong, because in so many other ways I was a good and caring husband, I justified what I did to myself.

"Upon being found out, my immediate reaction was to protect my wife, my children, my wider family, my work and my Other-Woman at all costs. Preventing upset and disruption to the status quo and the stability of everything in my life was my primary objective. It was not about shame or regret at that stage. The only regret was being foolish enough to get caught.

"For me, it was all about damage limitation and preventing my wife from being hurt any further, by her knowing as little of the detail as possible about the other relationship. However, my wife was hell bent on finding out every single little detail.

"I desperately wanted to prevent anything hurting my children and then there were further considerations like the potential impact on my job and so on. My ultimate goal was to protect everything dear to me, for as long as I possibly could, even as the evidence piled up against me.

"Only over time did the other emotions such as guilt, shame and regret begin to enter my mind. However, there was then a moment in time when the absolute need to protect the other women switched to trying to repair, rebuild and help my wife overcome the affair. This coincided with a desire to finally admit what I had done."

What we think about Alan's *script*

It is clear Alan was enjoying the connection he had with the Other-Woman as an antidote to the stresses he perceived he had in his marriage. Rather than develop the relationship with the Other-Woman, he should have communicated his unhappiness with his wife and given them both an opportunity to discuss their relationship and jointly found a solution. Instead of doing this he retreated into his "cosy, secret little world," which kept him away from the reality of life that includes, stress, pressure and the ups and downs in relationships. It takes strength not to run towards an escape route.

Alan saw the Other-Woman as "innocent" because his wife had "let him down" at times in their marriage. He clearly felt resentment about this and used it as justification for his developing relationship with the Other-Woman. It is shocking that his only regret was "being foolish enough to get caught."

Alan's wife is still with him and they are trying to work through it. Obviously, the stresses in the marriage weren't as bad as he thought!

Chris's story (and *script*)

Chris is a fifty-seven-year-old former Immigration Officer, now a security consultant living, in the South of England, married with three children.

"I think there is an in-built desire in men to mate and in a way, it drives them to perform like stag deer, not just in the rutting season, but throughout the whole year.

"It is part of nature, but in the modern world and the developed human brain, it leads some men to have to be the dominant male stag and attempt to mate with females almost on a continual basis.

"In this scenario, we could or even would, become serial adulterers. All that stops us are the boundaries, confines of society and the practicalities of actually doing it. I think this is particularly the case in Alpha male working environments, where there is also an abundance of female 'does' on tap.

"When I was younger, I was definitely one of those stags and despite the fact that morally I would try my best to avoid temptation, inside me, inside my brain, there was something that made me intent on bagging the most attractive girls for myself.

"This wasn't in a sexually predatory way, because if the girls didn't respond to my approaches I would back away and move on. I knew when I was getting the 'I'm not interested' signal, in the same way a doe sometimes gives a stag the same signal in the rutting season.

"I also had no desire to brag about my conquests, especially the secret ones and I found women appreciated that and trusted me as a consequence. It showed I respected them, which I did.

"My 'herd' wasn't as big as a stag's, but the female does that were part of my heard satisfied my inner needs.

"There were times when I tired of the inner drive to be the rampant, top stag and even in my youth, I longed for the day when, like the old deer with the largest antlers, I would be succeeded by the next generation of stags and I could settle into a quiet and happy family life.

"However, having once become a top stag, like the male deer in the rutting season in the month of October, it placed me in a vicious circle where I had to continually perform the role. This was both physically and mentally exhausting and yet at the same time, exciting and exhilarating.

"If there was a new girl at work and she was attractive and had a nice personality, I immediately had the urge to make her part of my herd and beat any of the other stags in securing her. This wasn't openly spoken about. It wasn't a declared competition with the other stags. In fact, I found the subtler I was about achieving my goal, the more likely I was to succeed.

"I never breached any confidences regarding any of the women in my herd, but some must have realised I had a tendency to play the field.

"One once said to me, 'We all know you love the girls, but you get away with it because you treat women well and have a cheeky smile.'

"In some ways, I found this a bizarre comment, because I would have thought that if the girls knew the way I was, it would put them off, but instead it quite often worked the other way.

"Again, I can only draw an analogy with nature and deer rutting, where the dominant stag somehow attracts the does, because nature drives the does to mate with the healthiest, strongest, most dominant male.

"This behaviour continued until I found a doe I fell in love with and then my pattern of behaviour would stop until I fell out of love or tired of her, and then off I would go again, back on the rutting routine. I deeply hurt some girls at that time and yet other girls have remained friends to this day, although my wife, quite rightly, won't allow me to continue those friendships now.

"Any man reading this will probably think, 'Wow, this guy had a great life.' Actually, it was the complete opposite. It was a curse, which has caused me great upset, sadness and disruption to what otherwise would have been a wonderful life. Although I was faithful when I first married, it did not last forever, and I reverted to 'rutting' in the end. I deeply regret being an Alpha stag and if I could change one thing in my life, it would be not to have this curse inflicted on me. (*It's interesting he refers to his sexual exploits as a curse, yet it is so obvious that his ego needed the constant reassurance that he was top stag. Winning his women confirmed his attractiveness to the opposite sex, putting all other competitors in their place.*)

"Although I think most men have the potential to be or want to be a top stag and a serial adulterer, for a variety of reasons they do not venture down that path. Perhaps some men simply do not work in an environment where there are other competing stags or indeed any 'does' to present opportunities?

"Some men do not have the personality, the cheeky smile or other attributes to attract the does but I also think that quite simply, some men are more decent than I was and are able to resist the inner urge and weakness.

"I am not proud of what I have done over the years and at times it has made my life miserable. I look back with deep regret regarding the hurt and damage I inflicted, not only on my wife, but also in my younger years on the women who were part of my 'herd.' I want to apologise to all those women for my behaviour.

"Looking back, it seems that throughout my rutting years I was constantly seeking happiness or something that I could not find. It is only since I aged and have effectively been deposed as a top stag, that I have finally found contentment in my life.

"The irony is, that the contentment was there all the time, with my wife and family. However, I still find it hard to totally break away from my past conquests and still keep some of them as my 'secret friends.' I don't know why I can't let them go, but I do know that my wife would see it as a further betrayal if she found out."

What we think about Chris's *script*
Doe a dear a female dear (or two or three or four or five or six!).
What was Chris on? Clearly a huge amount of testosterone!
You would be more inclined to accept this behaviour from a
man in his early years; playing the field, boosting his ego with
every conquest. We probably all know men like this. At least
Chris didn't boast about his conquests.

Chris said his behaviour continued until he found a doe
he fell in love with and then his pattern of behaviour would
stop until he fell out of love or tired of her, and then off he
would go again, back on the rutting routine. Sadly, this pattern
of behaviour never seemed to leave Chris's life even when he
was married.

Chris's *script* illustrates the 'because *he can, he does,*' which
indicates he lacks total commitment to one relationship at any
one time. Even when he got married, he followed the same
pattern; he fell in love—he tired of it—he started again.

Tom's story (and *script*)
Tom, a forty-five-year-old financial director, now works in the
charity sector, and is currently single. He lives in London.

"My partner thought I was having an affair with my office
secretary in Germany when I actually wasn't, we were just good
friends. Because we got on well I suppose there were signs that
aroused her suspicions.

"Eventually, however, we did have a relationship, but it
only lasted a few months. Then, not long before I was due to
return to England, the secretary asked me to give her a baby
before she was too old to have one. I felt bad about how I had
treated her, so I agreed to what I saw as an altruistic act. She

soon became pregnant and it was then that it dawned on me what I had done. *(As shocking as this is to read, it is more common than you think, remember Lisa's account in Chapter Three? It is clear that this relationship was far deeper than he would even have himself believe. Why did he feel bad about the way he had treated her? We strongly suspect the web of lies he weaved had actually trapped himself more than he knew).*

"For the first couple of months I did not know what to do. I did not tell anyone, but she had told two of her friends that I was the father. I had mixed emotions about what was happening.

"Everyone in the German company office, which was quite small, knew the secretary and I were very close. One of her friends, who knew I was the father, thought I should tell my partner. My Other-Woman also pressurised me to tell everyone in my family. I thought about it for a few weeks and eventually decided I had to tell my partner.

"It was the hardest thing I have ever had to do and I will never ever forget the look on my partner's face when I told her that the office secretary was pregnant by me. I had shattered her life and left her distraught in a foreign country, alone, without friends and family support.

"However, the worse thing of all was that I told my partner we actually hadn't had intercourse, but that I had agreed to help my secretary to have a baby and that as we would be returning to England soon, no one would know. I told my partner I had masturbated into a dish. The other woman then used the 'turkey baster' method to squirt the semen into her."

(He showed total disrespect for his partner in expecting her to believe

that although he had an affair with this woman, he chose to make her pregnant outside the act of sexual intercourse. Not only is it a blatant disregard for the impact this would have on his partner, but it appeared he thought it was more acceptable to tell her they didn't have sex to produce the baby!)

"Of course, my partner did not believe me. She was distraught and just couldn't comprehend what I had done, let alone forgive me. As a consequence, our relationship ended, my life has been ruined and so has that of my Other-Woman, who brings up our child alone."

Our response to Tom's *script*

Tom's *script* shows how he used the justification *script* for his actions towards the other woman as a way of alleviating his own guilt towards her, not to his partner. It would indicate that at some point in their relationship he had promised they would be together and this is what the other woman expected. When it actually became a reality, Tom clearly didn't want to commit, but was prepared to give her a baby, almost as a way of compensation. This would also help him alleviate some of the guilt he was feeling, but at no point did his partner seem to enter his mind in the decisions he took. It was all about him and the Other-Woman.

What have Alan, Chris and Tom got in common?

In simple terms Alan, Chris and Tom used the Justification, Denial and Blame *scripts* to excuse an affair. They all showed a capacity to lie, a desire for the thrill of secrecy and a need to be adored.

In trying to understand why these men have affairs it may

help you to think about the different parts of how our choices are made:

- I want.
- I want and it is not selfish.
- I want and it is selfish.
- I want and it's OK.
- I want and it is not OK.

The majority of men who have affairs appear to get what they want as a result of being selfish, knowing that it is not OK. Alan, Chris and Tom all had a desire, all knew what they wanted and then justified being selfish by making excuses and blaming their partners. However, in the end, they all accepted what they did was wrong and ultimately hurt others. The others are the ones who never figured in their decision to have an affair in the first place.

"She says it's really not very flattering to her that the women who fall in love with her husband are so uncommonly second-rate."

W. Somerset Maugham,
British playwright and novelist, 1874-1965

Chapter Six

His Other-Woman Script

After the revelations of the adulterer's Own *Script*, we now move on to discuss the lies he tells the Other-Woman, and you, to protect himself. We also address how you can handle these lies.

It would be easy for us to write about how many of the other women are heartless home-wreckers, selfish and manipulative. However, this is not always the case. Some of the other women don't realise they have been played and the person they have fallen in love with is married or in a relationship.

Some men are such accomplished pathological liars they can dupe anyone. You will recall that in Alan's account in the previous chapter, he openly admitted to protecting the Other-Woman and his secret 'cosy world.' He may even provide his wife with a made-up name for his Other-Woman to protect her identity.

One thing is almost certain: when most men are having an affair they choose to stop working on their existing relationship and instead put all their focus into the new and exciting part of their life. Making the Other-Woman feel like the number one person becomes their priority.

Without doubt, he will have made himself out to be a 'victim.' He will have no hesitation in telling the Other-Woman how you don't care about him and haven't had sex for months, even years. In essence, he will say nothing to show you in a good light.

By now the woman will be feeling sorry for him and want to take care of him, unlike you, the nasty vindictive psychopath who treats him like dirt. During the secretive stage of an affair, the Other-Woman is seen as exciting and full of mysterious fun.

Some men have told us it was the risk, danger and sense of excitement that held the appeal. Those of us on the receiving end of being cheated on will find this very hard to comprehend. While you are dealing with all the things everyday life brings to your door, he is looking for an escape from reality in his quest for a bit of fun.

When you find out your partner has cheated on you, you automatically react with anger, despair, humiliation, and total and utter confusion as your world falls apart. As a result, your behaviour may result in you showing signs of that 'erratic person' he has already told the Other-Woman you are. You may be crying one minute and screaming the next. Frankly, how did he expect you to behave when you found out?

The Other-Woman can often look like the saintly one, the one who is calm, listens, provides a shoulder to cry on and supports the man through the crisis they and your betraying partner actually caused in the first place!

It seems incredible that some women will fall for the clichés men have been saying for so long, but so many women continue to do so. This could be because, as women, we want to feel loved, attractive and wanted. In our opinion, we believe men want the same.

Let's remind ourselves of the *script* he is going to tell the Other-Woman about you and your relationship:

- She doesn't understand me.
- We live separate lives.
- We haven't had sex for years.
- I don't love her anymore.
- There is no romantic connection between us; we are like brother and sister.
- We are only together for the children.
- You are the most gorgeous woman I have ever known.
- I love you.
- I am going to leave her for you.
- She has betrayed me.

How far men will go to protect the Other-Woman

When discovered by their wives, some men will go to extraordinary steps to protect the Other-Woman. Here we share some stories and *scripts* so you can see for yourself.

Jeff's story (and *script*)

Jeff is a thirty-five-year-old journalist living in Texas with one child.

"I gave my wife false details about the woman I was having the affair with, including a made-up name and address, and a completely false story regarding everything about her. I tried as best as I could to throw my wife off the scent.

"For months, my wife researched the details I had given her, using search engines and other tools to confirm the accuracy of what I had told her. Deep down, I think she knew I had lied about who the Other-Woman was. She would not give up. Her pursuit of the Other-Woman was relentless and it made her ill.

"In the end, through slowly piecing all the evidence together, she told me who the woman was. I still tried to deny it, but in the end, she had worn me down and eventually the truth came out."

The male accounts we have included in The MAN*Script* probably do not sit comfortably with many of you reading this, but we have to appreciate their honesty, no matter how distasteful it is to us as women. There are no excuses. But for these men, it was the first time they had spoken about their affairs, so maybe seeing it down in black and white, they won't be able to avoid understanding what they did. . . and maybe they can change?

We asked some of the men we interviewed for Chapter Five, why they thought the women were prepared to enter into an affair? And why they had to protect them? Again, the answers are written in the men's own words.

Alan's response to *why?*

"It had started as an honest friendship and the Other-Woman was aware of all aspects of my life, because I had told her about my wife, my children and what I did at weekends. I had some knowledge of her life, but she was guarded about her relationship with her boyfriend, not opening up to me as much as I opened up to her.

"When the relationship moved from friendship to a sexual one, the Other-Woman in my life was adamant that she wouldn't do anything to damage my home life and insisted that what we were doing must remain secret. For obvious reasons, I was quite happy to go along with this.

"I was sure the person I was having the affair with clearly had feelings for me, but she was also very clinical about the rules of our relationship.

"When my wife discovered our affair, my Other-Woman was petrified about the ramifications and the impact on her own relationship, her family and her job. Despite all those fears, she was also genuinely ashamed of the damage she had inflicted on my wife and encouraged me to do all I could to repair things at home and salvage my marriage.

"She told me she had been a 'right bitch' and that she felt for my wife and what we had done to her. She had told me that our actions had been entirely selfish, that we had known it was selfish from the beginning and that we both knew it was wrong.

"I know some women reading this will say I am defending the person I had an affair with. I am not. I am just trying to relay the facts as they happened.

"Having vowed to my wife that the relationship was finished some months later, I communicated with my former Other-Woman again. I did it for what were the right reasons in my head, to clear something up, but that then led to more communication between us.

"Fortunately, my work pattern has since changed. I no longer have reason to visit her office, so there was no chance of physical contact again. In my head, it wasn't rekindling the affair, because there was no physical contact between us, but to my wife it was yet another betrayal. I am now fighting to save my marriage and this time I have learned my final lesson."

Chris' response to *why?*

"I think women who have an affair are as much a victim as the wives because I do not believe men are entirely honest about their home life or other factors. I was not always honest to the girls who were part of my herd, how could I be?"

The script he tells you and the Other-Woman, when he wants to reconcile your relationship

Julia Key's story, co-author of The MAN*Script*

"My husband and I were apart for nearly twelve months and in that time many lies were told to me. We all know how hard it is to break away from a long-term relationship, particularly if there is family involved and when the majority of that relationship had been good in the past.

"When my husband came back to see me, after everything had been publicised about his infidelity in the British newspapers, it was an odd scenario, but strangely comforting to see him. As he began to talk, quite ironically, I took on the role of his therapist rather than his wife. I listened to the story he told me and tried to help him work things out in his head.

"The following day he told me that he didn't want to be with the Other-Woman, that having read an early version of The MAN*Script*, he could see the writing on the wall and he realised he was making a fool of himself. He had been in nothing more than a fantasy relationship.

"With that in mind, he said he was going to make a telephone call to his Other-Woman, tell her that it was finished and that he wanted to be with me. I asked him to let me listen to that conversation, to prove to me that what he was saying was the truth. No prize in guessing, he wouldn't let me do that.

"Having told me so many lies, I wasn't going to believe him unless I heard it for myself. He wanted somewhere private to speak to her, where I would be unable to listen, so I encouraged him to talk to her in the car. Unbeknown to him, I had earlier placed a recording device in the car.

"I watched him talking to her as he sat in the car and the conversation must have lasted nearly fifteen minutes, after which he came back in the house. He told me how relieved he felt that he had told the Other-Woman he couldn't be with her because he loved me. He said he told her he had read The MANScript and their relationship was doomed to fail. I went to the car and got the recorder.

"What I heard on the tape was unbelievable; it was a completely duplicitous dialogue. The total opposite to what he had told me. He started off by saying that he would have to stay with me because my cancer was back; that he had proof and had seen the medical documents. He explained what a nightmare his family were and because of that he couldn't give her what she deserved. He couldn't fulfil all their dreams and the commitments that they had made to each other.

"He went on to say how much he loved her and he said this repeatedly.

"As the conversation continued, she understandably got quite irritated, angry and frustrated. With that, his tone began to change and he said to her, "I was going to come to you last night and you were right, maybe if I had, I wouldn't be feeling like I do today." Like many men, Richard, was probably trying to let the Other–Woman down gently, because of the guilt he would be feeling for hurting her and the possibility of keeping his options open.

"You can imagine how I felt and to be perfectly honest, with all that had gone on previously, I was very emotional. When he knew I had recorded him, he was extremely angry with me. He shouted at me, saying that he told her a load of rubbish just to get rid of her! He continued with this unbelievable tale, explaining that he had to let her down gently, but he didn't mean any of it. Then he said that all the upset was now my fault because I had recorded him and questioned him. He kept asking why I couldn't have just left it alone.

"It was unbelievable; Richard was no different to any other man trying to negotiate his way out of an affair."

Magda's story

Most affairs create a situation where there are lies, after lies, after lies and misery for everyone involved.

Magda, a forty-year-old, mother of three from Ghana, contacted our website. She was with her partner, Phil for thirteen years. During the last three years of their relationship he had an affair with a work colleague. He didn't want anyone to know what he had done, especially not his grown-up children from a previous relationship. The Other-Woman certainly didn't want her own husband to know and told Magda (when she confronted her), that he was very abusive, so she was terrified of what he would do if he found out.

What is worse is that when Magda was pregnant with her daughter, her partner told her, "When that fucking thing is out of your stomach, I am off."

How can any woman deal with that?

She said, "He told the Other-Woman that we had a sister and brother relationship and it had been like that for years —she believed him. I was pregnant, so how could she have bought that lie?"

Magda became so scared, nervous and anxious, that she kept his secrets and lies from other people. She even kept the Other-Woman's lies too, because she was worried that the Other-Woman would be in danger if her husband found out.

She told us, "I felt so alone, it took an enormous toll on my health, I developed severe depression, but was so scared about what would happen if I told anyone—they basically emotionally blackmailed me. I wore their deceit as if it were my own. After our daughter was born, he kept telling me that he loved me and had made a huge mistake, but I now realise that his version of love was a cruel and selfish one."

Despite the situation Magda found herself in and the pain that resulted from his affair, she told us that when he wanted to reconcile their relationship, she still loved him enough to try and make it work. He repeatedly told Magda that he had become trapped because the Other-Woman needed his support, but he told the Other-Woman that he had to stay with Magda because she couldn't cope alone with their young daughter, so it wasn't the right time to leave her.

Magda is now living alone with her three children.

"I became such a nervous wreck and started to think it was all my fault. I couldn't live in their 'dirty world' any longer, so decided to ask for help from my family and friends. As soon as I told people what had happened, I felt a great weight lift of my shoulders. I am so much happier now, I have my own front door and live my life for me, their cruel lies can't hurt me anymore."

A word of advice for the Other-Woman

This book is not about attacking or blaming you, the Other-Woman. However, if you are in a relationship with someone else's partner you need to bear in mind that the majority of women reading this book have been betrayed. They need to understand what makes a woman become the Other-Woman.

Sometimes, good people do bad things without intending to hurt other people.

However, there are also women who deliberately enter into an adulterous relationship, knowing what the consequences of being found out might be. There are other women who intentionally pursue a man who is already in a committed relationship. That woman may not care, because it is not her—but the wife—who will get hurt. That woman may even rationalise that if the wife can't keep her partner happy, then she deserves to be cheated on.

If you are the Other-Woman, you have most likely made a conscious decision to have an affair with someone who is married or in a relationship. You choose to allow the lies to flourish and you permit the man to deceive his partner.

An affair needs a marriage/partnership to keep its excitement and sense of fun. It is not reciprocal: a marriage/partnership does not need an affair to thrive and survive. If he was so unhappy and not understood, why didn't he end the marriage *before* he met you? Probably because the marriage has something an affair can never have—reality.

By getting involved with a man who is already married or in a committed relationship you are automatically involved with a man who lies. There is very little doubt that he is almost certainly lying to his wife and you have become part of that betrayal. Do not be fooled into thinking that he will not also be lying to you.

If you are taken in by his words of 'I've never met anybody like you before, I love you so much, I know we are meant to be together. I cannot leave my wife at the moment, but I will when the time is right, please wait for me' then you are naïve, gullible and deluded. By believing that he is telling you the truth, you are setting yourself up to be another victim of his lies. This is a very poor basis for a trusting relationship to begin and survive.

For whatever reason, when we are in love with someone, we want to believe everything they are telling us. You cling on to their every word so that in your mind it reinforces their feelings for you. The problem with this is that quite often his behaviour tells a different story. This applies to both the Other-Woman and the partner who is being betrayed.

What works as an affair, may not work as a full-time relationship. All the excitement is gone. You will no longer see the clean, attentive, adoring side of him, but the dirty socks and his weaknesses. You also have proof of what he is capable of; the very real knowledge that if a man can cheat on his wife/partner, he can/will cheat on you.

The betrayed wife/partner was once regarded by her partner as gorgeous, exciting, fun-loving and she listened to his every word too. When he says he is unhappily married and his wife doesn't understand him, tell him to go home, cherish what he has and talk to his wife/partner. If he really values and loves you, and his home relationship is really at an end, he will do the decent thing at home and come back to you.

The Other-Woman should be aware that many men told us they had no intention of leaving their wives/partners. The love for their partner had not actually diminished, in fact, their greatest fear was losing their partner. Many said that once they were found out and their partner refused to have them back, the attachment became stronger, not because of wanting to be with the Other-Woman, but because of a fear of being alone.

What many of us may struggle with is the fact that many men said they considered their home relationships to be happy but justified their guilt by telling the Other-Woman they were unhappy.

Finally, we were shocked when we spoke to one of the Other-Women who told us they had been aware of their father's betrayal of their mother. They witnessed the devastating affect it had on their mother, yet it didn't stop them from pursuing a relationship with a married or attached man.

To summarise, in the words of Lisa, one of the many amazing women who contacts us regularly on our website, "You bagged yourself a cheater."

Remember. . .

- Beware that his behaviour often tells a different story to his words.
- Remember sometimes good people do bad things without intending to hurt other people.
- An affair needs a marriage/partnership to keep its excitement and sense of fun. It is not reciprocal: a marriage/partnership does not need an affair.
- The Other-Woman may not know she is having a relationship with someone already in a partnership, but if they do, they are actively permitting the lies and deceit to continue.
- Some men will go a long way to protect the 'Other-Woman'.

"The moment there is suspicion about a person's motives,
everything he does becomes tainted."

Mahatma Ghandi,
India independent movement leader, 1869–1948

Chapter Seven

Understanding The Adulterer

As women, we tend to spend a lot of time thinking about what has happened, but also trying to understand or give reason to another's motives and actions. Understanding the adulterer may not be on your agenda right now, but this section will help to better understand some of the potential reasons pertaining to an age-old question: why do men cheat?

Why men cheat

We wish we had a penny for every time a woman has asked us this. It is a long-standing question that nobody has the definitive answer to. What we do know is that thousands of women say, "Why didn't he talk to me and tell me how he felt?"

Communication is a key factor, whether it is communication with your partner or his own internal communication. There are a few reasons why men cheat, but the two main ones tend to be:

- There is fault in their relationship.
- There is a fault within themselves.

The first is fairly straightforward. Affairs fulfil some need that isn't being met within the long-term relationship and continues to be unmet. The adulterer wants to maintain the equilibrium of the main relationship but looks elsewhere for the things he perceives to be missing.

The second reason is more complex because there may be deep-rooted issues within the individual that are not resolved. In our experience, these issues are often connected to the mother and son relationship and/or other childhood experiences. There may also be an addiction to the feelings of excitement and power.

Fear and excitement can consume the adulterer—until they are found out. When that happens, suddenly the 'rock' of a relationship with the wife or partner is threatened and the cry 'I'll never do it again,' can be heard from the rooftops!

This is a crucial point in the adulterer's life. If he is prepared to look at himself and explore his deeper issues, there is real hope of change. If he isn't, then you can expect him to carry on having affairs, regardless of the furious protestations to the contrary.

Flaws in the relationship can be worked on, particularly with the help of joint counselling. Flaws within his personality are much harder to fix. If the adulterer accepts and acknowledges there may be underlying issues that are motivating his behaviour, there is also hope for that relationship too. In this situation, we strongly recommend talking therapy, ideally with a counsellor. This can be expensive but an alternative is to seek help via your doctor.

Understand the adulterer's mind

Many men who cheat have a capacity to lie to anyone, even to themselves! The majority of women say it is just about the sex when men cheat, but many researchers have claimed that it is actually about a man's emotional needs, rather than a sexual driver or trigger.

However, the sexually explicit texts many of us have seen on our partner's telephones makes all that hard to believe. This is probably how they manage to tell themselves that it is OK, because it is about having their emotional needs stroked (in other words their egos) rather than just their sexual needs. We discuss this further in Chapter Nine: Challenging Scenarios And Personal Storms, where we explore why men cheat at a time when their women needed them the most.

One thing that is clearly part of their *script* is the way most men are able to compartmentalise their world. They can view their life in various boxes: work box, home box, social box, sports box. Each box is detached from each of the other boxes.

Women, on the other hand, also have many roles—the wife, the mother, the carer, the career woman and so on—but these roles tend to cross over. Women don't view each aspect as a separate compartment or box. Each aspect of a woman's life impacts, or is intertwined with, the others.

The sixty-six-million-dollar question, "Will he change?"

The answer to this is in his past actions. Usually, a person's past behaviour will give you a fairly accurate assessment of their future actions. You can assume they will not change unless they seek professional help to modify their behaviour. This is particularly applicable if a man continually displaces blame onto other people, when he is clearly the person at fault.

Most importantly, before we talk about the adulterer, do

not let the Other-Woman or ex-partner make you think you are any less of a person because of what they have done. In fact, you need to start telling yourself the exact opposite and quickly. It may reassure you to know that men often 'cheat down.' By that we mean he rarely cheats with a woman who is as attractive as the one he currently has.

Interestingly enough, this is backed up by several studies, including research by relationship counsellor M. Gary Neuman, author of 'The Truth About Cheating.' He interviewed two hundred men about the reasons why they felt the need to cheat. A staggering eighty-eight percent of men said that the affair partner was no more physically attractive than their wife/partner.

Men usually cheat for sex, or so women think, but it can also be for attention, adoration, something that feeds their ego to know they still 'have it', whatever *it* might be. Some men will say it was for emotional reasons and some will just say *because I could.*

Many of the men we spoke to openly admitted being totally 'infatuated' by the woman they had an affair with. They said they became consumed with a passion for someone, even though they knew it was risky, but they could not stop the desire.

When a man becomes infatuated with another woman, this is known as limerence; *'A state of mind, which results from a romantic attraction to another person and typically includes obsessive thoughts and fantasies and a desire to form or maintain a relationship with the object of love and to have those feelings reciprocated.'*

Sex is central to the initial stages of being infatuated with someone. Debs, a thirty-one-year-old physiotherapist from

Canada, told us that her father used to say, "When the dickie becomes hard, the brain becomes soft."

Lust is a romantic infatuation, which men feel for their Other-Woman, but it is the love he feels for his wife/partner that keeps many couples together after the infatuation for the Other-Woman has long faded.

Men can become completely blinded by infatuation. It doesn't matter what other people tell them about the Other-Woman or try to convince them that they are destroying their lives; they can't see it. We often hear women say, "Why can't he see the real her?"

However, it is also really important to protect yourself and never underestimate how determined some women are to see the relationship with his wife/partner destroyed.

Maddie, a thirty-nine-year-old mother of three from Cheshire, told us that her husband asked to talk to her when their children were out at a friend's house. She said, "I just knew what he was going to tell me. My gut instinct had been screaming at me, but I was already at the lowest point in my life, having discovered my husband's affair six months previously. He sat me down and before the words came out of his mouth, I said 'she is pregnant, isn't she?' to which he started crying and said yes.

"I honestly cannot remember anything else about that conversation. I went into total shock and literally couldn't breathe. I recall him telling me that she had been pushing him to tell me and she knew when he was going to do it.

"I really cannot remember anything else for most of the day except in the evening I drank a whole bottle of wine in minutes. I was so enraged, I telephoned her. I remember swearing at her and telling her she had destroyed a family. I was screaming and crying. She was expecting my call and had her sister with her, who came on the phone and called me a psychopath, amongst other cruel things.

"What I hadn't expected was that as she knew I was going to call her, she had a tape recorder ready and recorded our conversation.

"The next day I received a call from the police telling me to report to the station, where I would be questioned under caution for harassment and threatening behaviour. I have never been so scared in all my life. I had never walked into a police station before and I was terrified. I also couldn't believe how another woman could be so cruel and calculating in her desire to hurt me.

"At the station, I was so distressed that I wet myself in fear. I had been given the worst news of my life and I couldn't breathe properly because of the pain I felt, yet this Other-Woman was intent of seeing me on my knees!

"To this day I cannot comprehend the level of cruelty she showed me and when I drive past the police station I still feel sick, reliving the worst time of my life. I know one thing for certain, she was determined to get him and she was not going to let me, his wife stand in her way."

Maddie's eyes were filled with tears as she told us her story, but she suddenly sat bolt upright and without hesitation said, "I swore I would never cry another tear over what they did to me. I am in a much better place now than I ever was and I know that what I dealt with then has made me the strong person I am today. My life is so much better because of it. I used to think if ever I met her in the street, I would want to slap her, but now I know that I would just walk past with my head held high, as she is totally insignificant to me."

Men often have a distorted version of the woman they are involved with. He has to transform her into someone really special to justify the risk to his relationship/marriage. All these thoughts and distortions are great in the beginning but are unlikely to last long term. If the relationship lasts long enough, the likelihood is that reality will eventually settle in. Fantasy is exciting, but reality is not. It is highly unlikely that in an affair situation you truly know everything about each other. You have to be in a long-term relationship to really know someone.

Real love is about knowing the good and the bad, their attributes and their flaws and loving them in their entirety. Real love comes when you hang on in there, when the going gets tough and you don't look for a way out. A relationship that is built on deception, while also deceiving another, is born out of a fantasy. For a time, it is fun and exciting, but when the guilt kicks in, reality comes calling.

This can be experienced on both sides of the betrayal.

Grace, a fifty-one-year-old teacher from Bristol, told us that her husband's Other-Woman, who was also fifty-one, was terrified of her own partner finding out. She didn't care that his wife had been destroyed by their affair, but she didn't want her own life and relationship with her partner destroyed!

Grace said, "I could not comprehend how she thought it was OK to destroy my life and my family and put me through hell, but she did not want her life to be impacted in the same way—unbelievable! I agreed not to tell her partner after my husband pleaded with me, but now I live with that regret every day and the deceitful fact that she carried on as though nothing had happened. It was one rule for me and one for her!"

Addictive love

Addictive love is like being completely carried away by an unrealistic, all-consuming passion. When someone is having an affair their feelings for the other person can become very addictive. The chemicals that the brain releases are similar to those from heroin, cocaine or other addictive drugs. Ending any addiction can be extremely difficult. Asking an alcoholic not to drink can only be achieved with total abstinence and it is the same with an affair. If a man wants to reconcile his relationship with his partner there has to be total abstinence from the third party. This means no further contact whatsoever.

It may help to see your partner as an alcoholic who is in recovery. He craves the excitement of the affair and how it made him feel. Like any other addiction, there is a period of withdrawal and like any withdrawal there is always the temptation to 'use' again.

This is a really hard thing for you to understand, as the victim of an affair. It means that your partner still has feelings for the Other-Woman and while those feelings remain, your relationship still feels under threat. This helps to explain the need you may feel to repeatedly ask your partner how he feels about the Other-Woman. You are seeking reassurance to reduce the feelings of anxiety you have. You are worried that there is a temptation for him to resume the affair.

If a man is prone to cheating, he will find any excuse to do so. To have two women in his life can be a reflection of an underlying insecurity. It is a bit like being a child (the man) needing the safety of his mother (the wife/partner), while he enjoys the excitement of his friend (the Other-Woman). The excitement can only be truly experienced if the safety of the mother (wife/partner) is also guaranteed. Without this, the affair is too fearful because the man knows subconsciously that it has the capability to destroy him. The threat of destruction creates the overwhelming need to deny. In other words, he cannot cope with instability.

Men, who have issues with control, are more likely to need a stable environment in which to conduct an affair. Men who may have been born into a domineering and controlling childhood and where rules played a potent part of their upbringing, may seek to free themselves from this control by embarking on serial affairs, free from the rules that come from being in a relationship.

If your husband/partner has an affair and you are undecided whether you want to stay with him or not, your partner may find it even more difficult to give up the Other-Woman. His need for emotional security has to come from someone and it is at this point that the role becomes reversed; the Other-Woman becomes the stability and the wife becomes the one he craves. This situation creates such fear in the man because his emotional security is being threatened. He may not let go of the Other-Woman until he is sure that the wife/ partner will take him back.

Many women find this scenario totally unacceptable, but if it can be understood from an emotional-need perspective, it may help the woman to understand that the affair is not about love. It can be likened to a child playing with its favourite toy. Like all favourite 'boys toys' he may want to keep his 'favourite' to go back to for security but he can and will play with other toys at the same time.

This pattern will continue regardless of how many affairs he might have.

Understand the adulterer's personality

If a man has cheated only once and has learnt his lesson, then it shows the strength of his character. If a man cheats more than once, he is likely to repeat this pattern and that shows a flaw in his character.

The personality traits that may cause a man to cheat are sometimes in contradiction. Some men will have high self-esteem and be your typical alpha male. Other men will be the exact opposite and in need of reaffirming their identity within the concept of their own insecurities.

If you have been in a relationship for many years and are suddenly seeing a side of the man you love that you have never seen before, here is why. . .

There are many facets to a person's personality that we are unaware of. Unfaithful men may be unaware of their capacity to lie until they are faced with a situation that evokes a side to them they themselves have possibly never seen before. Let's not forget being in an affair is a secret situation. Secrets require certain devious and manipulating behaviours, along with a convincing ability to lie.

If this is your partner's first affair, then he too might be surprised at the way he has behaved. If your partner has done this before, then this can be a pattern of behaviour that is deep-rooted within his personality.

If this is your first experience of betrayal, then your reaction may also bring out a side to your personality that you didn't even know you had. You may feel such extreme anger that it shocks you; seeking out revenge in ways you never thought possible. You may feel so hurt and immobilised that you find it hard to function. This is normal. Do not forget that your personality is going to play a really big part in how you handle the effect of his affair.

Is it a family thing?

How many times have you heard someone say, "Like father like son?" Probably many, but the old adage is sadly often true when it comes to adultery.

In 2011, researchers decided to put this theory to the test and concluded that a man who has a cheating father, is twice as likely to cheat as one who didn't.

"No!" I can hear you screaming, yet another excuse a cheating man has been given to justify his cheating.

"It's in my genes, there is nothing I can do about it!"

Scientists from Charles University in Prague, Czech Republic, found that men are more likely to be unfaithful if their fathers had been. In a study of eighty-six couples, the researchers noted both men and women cheated on their partners, but women did not seem to be as influenced by their parents' unfaithfulness.

The lead researcher, Jan Haverlick, suggested that this might be because sons of cheating fathers see their father's actions and see them get away with it. What they undoubtedly also saw was the devastating impact of their father's infidelity on their mothers, yet many still repeat the same mistakes with their own partner and family.

In 2015, Dr Dana Weiser Ph.D. from Tech University in Texas, United States, surveyed people regarding their parents' relationship and infidelity and their personal relationships. Nearly half of those surveyed whose parents had cheated, admitted to having cheated on a partner, making them *twice* as likely to stray as those brought up in a faithful family.

We suggest that if it is in his genes, he has been forewarned and should be going out of his way to ensure that he doesn't repeat his father's behaviour. He should be talking to you about the strength of your relationship and making sure he doesn't make the same mistakes his father made.

Remember. . .

- He is likely to blame you and will attempt to convince you that it is your fault. It is not!
- If he is prepared to look at himself and explore his deeper issues, there is a real hope of change.
- Research shows that sons of men who cheated on their partners are twice as likely to cheat on their wife/partner. However, it doesn't have to be this way. Men can instead work on ensuring they don't repeat their father's behaviour by increasing communication with their partner and discussing their concerns.
- If your partner genuinely wants to reconcile, he has to get rid of the other woman forever—that means zero contact of any kind.
- If a man cheats more than twice, he is more likely to continue to cheat.

"Don't let someone else's opinion of you become your reality."

Les Brown,
American author and motivational speaker

Chapter Eight

His Other People Script

An affair can have repercussions on a wider scale than within your immediate family unit. It can permeate into the lives of other family members, friends and colleagues. He may even have been telling them a different *script* to the one he was telling you and himself, and the Other-Woman. In this chapter we will discuss the ricochet affect his affair has on your family and those close to you. We will also offer damage-limitation guidance and support. Please also refer to our website www. keys2life.co.uk and My Freedom Diary.

What he tells other people
- It is not what it seems.
- She has got it all wrong.
- My life has been very difficult for a long time.
- We live totally separate lives.
- She has betrayed me (e.g. had an affair, lies, is an alcoholic or spends all my money).
- She told me our relationship/marriage was finished, that is why I continued the affair.
- People are stirring up trouble, saying things that aren't true.

Work colleagues

The work environment is considered to be the number one place for infidelity to take shape, probably because opportunities to ignite an affair are available, such as overnight trips and meetings. Some men can face losing their jobs if it becomes known that they have been having an affair. That is what happened to Tom. (Tom appeared earlier in The MAN*Script* talking about his time working in Germany—you may remember him as 'the guy who gave the turkey baster account'.)

Fear of losing his job or credibility in his workplace can be reasons why men justify the secrecy and feel they need to keep their other relationship hidden. If your partner has had an affair with a work colleague, it can make for a very difficult situation with his job. Many men will continue to deny, deny and deny; to prevent their employers from finding out. They may also feel responsible for the precarious situation the Other-Woman now finds herself in.

Children

It is really important to consider the effect on children following infidelity. If you have children, you must tread very carefully. Even if neither of you tell the children about the affair, there will be tension between you and they will pick up on this. A child who is old enough to understand what infidelity means may feel anger, shame and resentment. If children carry the burden of shame, they can learn to feel guilty and blame themselves.

Children very quickly lose their sense of security when they see and hear the two people they love most shouting and arguing. They may feel torn, because they love both parents equally. They may also feel they have to dislike the parent who cheated and this can lead to extreme anxiety and distress.

In some children, these heightened levels of anxiety can lead to sleep disorders and bed-wetting. In other children, this may present with behavioural difficulties, school refusal or regression in learning.

Never be tempted to tell your children what a 'shit' their Dad is. They don't need to know this.

Paula, a forty-three-year-old artist from Guildford in Surrey, spoke candidly about how she was so angry with her husband that she told her son what he had done. She regrets this every day of her life and her husband then used this in his *script* to tell everyone what sort of person she 'really' was and how this led him to continue with the affair.

Nadia, a fifty-six-year-old accountant from Cheltenham, said her sixty-year-old husband told her that he had an affair when he was with his previous wife, when their daughter was seven years old. He thought everyone had got through it and moved on. However, sixteen years later his relationship with his daughter completely broke down and he realised it was because of the affair he had so long ago. His daughter internalised the pain—'acting in'—and had been suffering, without his knowledge, for many years in silence.

We urge men who are thinking about having an affair to talk with their partners before they embark on this treacherous journey because the damage to their extended families, especially their children, can be long lasting. The impact will be felt by a much wider circle of people than simply the two involved in the affair and the betrayed partner.

Effect on family and friends

Many relationships today are second time around and with those relationships come children. Dealing with a betrayal and trying to put on a brave front for your partner's children can be a recipe for disaster (for you not them). If your partner has left you, he too may be facing a situation like the one we are about to describe. Your partner needs to read this section, because this is what could lay ahead of him but he doesn't yet know it.

Men need to be really careful with what they tell friends, family and their wider circle because this can impact on everyone's future relationship, whether you separate or stay together. When infidelity is discovered, family and friends can have very strong opinions and their influence can become toxic. If it is not the first time it has happened, you may be reluctant to confide in them for fear of being judged.

Friends and family can also grieve the loss of your relationship and feel angry about it. After all, it impacts on them too and can cause strained situations at family gatherings. Let's not forget about grandparents, who in some cases may never see their grandchildren again!

What is worse is that some parents see this as an opportunity to actively break up their son or daughter's marriage or relationship, particularly if they don't like their spouse or partner. Other parents see this as a time to enable the adulterer to carry on their behaviour, by excusing it, especially if he had been—in their eyes—the perfect child who could do no wrong. They may also follow his *script* and justify his actions for him, enabling him to have the affair as it makes him 'happier.' We have heard from women who have said the same of their partner's sibling/s, who even befriend the Other-Woman in order to influence their brother's choices.

This was the case for Flick, a twenty-one-year-old student from Manchester. She told us that her boyfriend's sister always resented her, so when he started seeing someone else behind her back, his sister pushed him to carry on with the relationship, even though he said he wanted to be back with Flick.

When an affair is out in the open, family friends and colleagues consciously or unconsciously choose sides. We all know couples who have separated and friends who have joined either *his* or *her* camp.

True friends will love and support you, whatever decision you make in life. Some friends, though, develop such strong opinions about who is right and who is wrong, that the friendship is irrevocably affected.

Eve, a thirty-five-year-old Personal Assistant from York and mother of two, spoke to us about how she lost most of her circle of friends because her husband was so convincing with his version of events and the reasons why he needed the Other-Woman.

Rose, a thirty-seven-year-old PR executive from Berkshire, told us how she had lived in the same area for most of her life where her husband was quite influential in the community. He made up all sorts of reasons why he needed to have an affair. When she went to her local pharmacist to buy toiletries, they refused to serve her.

Men who are close to or influenced by their mothers are particularly worried about what she may think. He may tell her derogatory things about you, especially if you have a close relationship to her. No mother wants to think that her son is capable of infidelity. As they say, 'Blood is thicker than water.'

This is a hard situation to deal with because you are the one who has been let down badly and may find yourself having to put the record straight.

Jane, a twenty-six-year-old, charity worker from Norwich, told us that her mother-in-law accused her of trapping her son into marriage in the first place, by deliberately getting pregnant.

The aftermath of infidelity when there are stepchildren

Kate is a divorced woman in her forties from Columbia whose ex-husband was having an affair. She told us how he would leave her to be with the Other-Woman during the week, only coming back every weekend to pretend to be a happy family for the sake of his three children from his previous relationship. He didn't want his children to know what he had done and was so terrified of them finding out and thinking badly of him.

Kate said, "I was really concerned about how they would react as they had already suffered badly from the breakup of their parents' marriage, so I played along with his pretence for the sake of his children. Naturally I started to resent the way he spoke to and treated his children, compared to the way he spoke to me. I became nervous, anxious, and was totally, heartbroken, struggling to cope. On top of this, I had post-natal depression, following the birth of our daughter and felt totally unsupported by him."

It was such a terrible time for Kate that she was later diagnosed with PTSD, brought on by the situation he had put her in. As a consequence, Kate said, "I lost who I was and allowed myself to become a 'victim'."

You can only become a victim if you see yourself as one.

Yes, you may have been cheated on or fooled by someone else, but you have it in you to take control back and move forward in your life.

Sadly, Kate is now estranged from her stepchildren and it appears that they had known what was going on all along. Her step-daughter told her that it was 'pathetic and boring.' Kate had tried so hard to be a good step-mum to them, but sadly they did not see it that way.

We are telling you Kate's story because we want you to realise how important it is to be true to yourself and not to allow yourself be bullied by a man's lack of respect for you; coupled with his desire to be seen as perfect to his children. If he can't be honest with his family, then take yourself out of the situation. Such emotional turmoil will destroy you if you don't.

Kate struggled to keep going through all the hurt she was dealing with, she said, "I put on a brave front but they have no respect for me for doing that."

They told her, "We walked on egg shells."

How on earth do they think she felt?

She said, "I should have remained true to myself, not everyone else. I tried to protect the status quo for everyone, but now realise it was the wrong thing to do, especially for my own wellbeing."

We can't stress this point enough. If you find yourself in a similar situation, we advise you seek professional help or talk to someone you can trust. Do not deal with it alone.

Protecting his reputation

It is important to remember that men will behave badly towards you, but they hate the thought of anyone knowing what a shit they really are. Infidelity not only impacts on you, but on the wider family and circle of friends. Your husband/partner may use any excuse in his *script* to protect his reputation and justify his betrayal, especially to family. He may not even have any hesitation in telling your family what a bad person you are!

What also happens quite regularly and comes as quite a surprise to the person who has been cheated on, is that they themselves will often defend their betraying partner to other people! It is as though we are scared of being judged for making such a bad choice in a man.

How many times have we heard friends who have been cheated on say, "Well, he is really kind in other ways," or something like, "He has been under enormous stress."

We are sure you have and it is even more common when there are children involved because no woman likes to think the man she has had children with is actually a nasty, narcissistic, liar. Women who contact us on our website, regularly defend their cheating partners.

Patricia, a forty-one-year-old financial advisor from South London, said, "Last year I discovered my husband had been having an affair with a married woman for the last three years.

"I met with some friends and my sisters for dinner and as I poured my heart out to them, they all said how much they had always disliked him and he wasn't good enough for me. After berating him myself, I actually felt really angry when they started on him and I found myself telling them about his difficult childhood and how he had struggled for years to get over what had happened to him.

"They all looked at me shocked and asked why I was now defending him? I couldn't answer. I thought it was because I still loved him, but I think maybe it was because it reflected badly on me, maybe I had made a bad choice. I am so confused about how I felt."

The best mate's dilemma

Throughout our research for this book, we were surprised how many men spoke to us frankly about how their friend's affair had impacted on their own families.

James, a forty-five-year-old taxi driver from Brighton, spoke about how his best friend's affair had caused a rift between him and his wife. He had immense loyalty to his best friend, but also felt under pressure to support his wife.

As two couples, they had been extremely close, enjoying holidays and time together. When his friend had an affair and the marriage ended, his wife could no longer tolerate him seeing his lifelong best friend. His friend's wife had told them one version of events and his friend had told them a different version. This caused such animosity between the best friend and his wife that their own marriage started to fall apart.

Remember. . .

- Be true to yourself and don't let yourself be bullied by a man's lack of respect for you.
- Do not be afraid to ask for professional help or talk to someone you trust.
- Be aware that people will 'take sides' after an affair becomes public. True friends will stick by you.
- Friends and family may also grieve the loss of your relationship.
- Be mindful that some people you know may have a hidden agenda when giving you advice—be vigilant.

"No one makes you feel inferior without your consent"

Eleanor Roosevelt,
American politician, diplomat and activist, 1884-1962

Chapter Nine

Challenging Scenarios And Personal Storms

There are many common scenarios in modern society that can make being cheated on even more difficult to deal with. It is hard to know whether or not the scenarios we talk about in this chapter are really more common today than in previous years, or whether they have always been prevalent, but not so visible, accepted or spoken about?

We will consider scenarios that appear to give rise to men having affairs and how they can impact on you as a woman. Actual reality is hard to gauge because some of the life-changing events we describe, such as pregnancy, are such an emotional time for women that they are reluctant to talk openly.

We will discuss many of the life-changing situations that impact on us as women, causing us to go through what we refer to as 'personal storms.' It is bad enough having to deal with storms such as the menopause or ill health, without the additional burden of your partner's infidelity. It is often a time when we need our partner the most that they let us down.

We also examine the older man/younger woman scenario, which impacted on co-author of The MAN*Script*, Julia.

Age is but a number

Let us make it very clear that it doesn't matter whether you are eighteen or eighty, the emotional impact of betrayal is usually the same. Your age is irrelevant. It is how you think about yourself in relation to that age that can affect how you deal with the fallout from an affair. Do you define yourself by how old you are? Or are you the type of person for whom age is but a number and your life experiences, not your age, makes you the person you are today?

Being cheated on evokes a strong feeling of rejection. For some people, rejection is a huge core issue. It is something you can become more vulnerable to because of past relationship issues.

This is when you may start to question your attractiveness, your personality, your self-worth, your identity and the role you have played in your previous relationships.

Older man, younger woman

Many women have contacted us via our website www.keys2life. co.uk because their partner has left them for a younger woman. It is for this reason that we have chosen to discuss the dynamics of a large age-gap relationship.

What we have written is by no means the definitive explanation for why a younger woman is attracted to an older man, but it gives some insight into the possibilities as to why large age-gap scenarios appear to be happening on a more regular basis.

Of course, there are age-gap relationships that work really well and the couple involved are blissfully happy, but these tend to be the exception rather than the rule. Usually, those that do succeed don't start out as a result of an affair.

If your partner has left you for a younger woman, then the fears we talk about may well be exacerbated by the delusion that you are less of a person because you are older. That is simply not true. In fact, the opposite is true.

Think about it for a moment, remember yourself at a similar age. Yes, the body may have been more 'intact,' but the mind certainly wasn't. Your ability to handle life events would have been far more of a challenge then than it is now.

In Julia's personal experience, she was asked many times if it was worse for her because her husband had repeatedly cheated on her with a younger woman. She states quite categorically and with complete honestly that it was absolutely not the case, "I would have felt more personally threatened by a woman of a similar age to me."

But, what is it about the older man that makes them attractive to younger women? We live in an era in which many young people have witnessed the breakup of their parent's relationship. From a young woman's perspective, her father leaving the family home for another woman could cause her to form the view that the woman who has taken her father away is more special than she (his daughter) is.

For a young girl, the dynamics of such a relationship is incredibly threatening to her own identity. To have your father leave your mother for somebody else not only betrays your mother, but it also betrays you, the child. The father-daughter relationship can create the foundation for the daughter's future relationships. It may influence the type of man she chooses.

Is it any wonder, through her vulnerability and need for the attention of an older man, that she may seek the company of older men? By doing so, she may be seeking the security that she felt was lost or possibly never had when her own father left the family home.

It is not uncommon for the need or desire for security to be perceived as love and that type of love plays to the man's ego.

The older man invariably seeks to make the younger woman feel special and by doing this, he is playing—sometimes subconsciously—to her need for recognition and to be wanted.

This type of relationship can be hugely seductive for both the man and the woman. After all, there is nothing more powerful to the ego of a man than to be needed and desired. There is also nothing more alluring to a younger woman than a man who is in a powerful position who can provide her with the recognition she craves. It is an alluring aphrodisiac, but one based on naivety.

Young women have grown up in a culture of immediate response and gratification—social media being a prime facilitator of this. Young women today appear to know what they want and have more determination to acquire it than those who were brought up in previous generations. Gone are the days when derogatory comments would be made about any woman who made it clear what she wanted or desired from a man. Today it is accepted that women are equal in the relationship stakes and women can make the first move in a way society did not permit them to do twenty years ago.

If we take this as the case, does it mean that there are greater numbers of younger women available to older men? Similarly, does a changing society no longer view an older man-younger woman relationship in the negative way it once did?

Personality traits and ego figure highly when determining who and who will not engage in this dynamic. Men's ego can be so strong that it blinds them to the consequences of pursuing the attentions of another woman. The fear of getting older is something that can also really affect men, far more than women might think.

Paul, a fifty-seven-year-old IT Consultant from Amsterdam, married for nineteen years, told us that it was the energy and excitement of a younger woman that attracted him to her. He felt it gave him back something he was rapidly losing in his own life, as he aged. He said, "She made me feel alive again and I could escape reality when I was with her."

Not all men will succumb to such desires, but for those who do, it often ends in tears. Once again, the reality is hidden by a fantasy, which does not allow them to see the truth or consequence of their actions.

Statistically, large age-gap relationships, which start out as affairs, do not last and if they do, it is the man who tends to become the most discontented. He increasingly experiences the pressure and responsibility of the situation.

What the younger woman doesn't realise, particularly when there are children involved from previous relationships, is that eventually she is faced with the reality of sharing the life with the adulterous man, which may not turn out as she expected. In the end, she may be competing for attention with his children, some of whom will be older or the same age as her. This may not be very easy for a young woman to accept and invariably, it causes conflict.

However, sometimes it works the other way around.

Michael, a wealthy man in his sixties from Surrey, started a relationship with an eighteen-year-old girl. All was good at first, but then the eighteen-year-old girlfriend began to spend more time on the PlayStation with his son from his previous marriage, rather than wanting to be with him. He ended up being jealous of his thirteen-year-old son!

Why some women end up with younger men

Age-gap relationships are on the rise—with more women choosing to date significantly younger men. You only have to look at the example of Monsieur Macron, the President of France, whose wife is twenty-five years older. In Hollywood pairings, Eva Mendes is six years older than Ryan Gosling. However, it could be argued that this is nothing new—older women dating younger men has been happening for years. What is interesting, however, is society's interest in this concept versus what is seen as 'normal practice' when an older man dates a younger woman. As women, we are feeling more empowered and confident in the choice of partner we make. Age is not a concerning factor.

When Macron and Bridgett Trogneux first began their relationship in 1993, he was a fifteen-year-old still at school and she his teacher. At the time of their initial affair, Bridgette Trogneux was married with three children one of whom was in the same school class as Macron. That certainly had tongues wagging in the quiet middle-class town of Amiens! Nearly twenty-five years later, modern French society now accepts their relationship and almost without question. However, in the UK, headlines such as 'French Kiss: How French election front-runner Emmanuel Macron, thirty-nine, seduced gran, sixty-four, who he fell for at FIFTEEN,' show there is some way to go in terms of societal acceptance of the older woman–younger man partnership.

It begs the question, if *he* had been the older partner, would it have received any comment at all?

According to the UK magazine Saga, wider age group relationships are on the rise, with more women choosing to date significantly younger men. Research by the University of Canada discovered that older women, who have previously been married, are now deliberately looking for relationships with younger men.

According to a study published in Psychology of Women Quarterly, as quoted in Saga Magazine, February 2017, older women who are at least a decade older than their partners, report being happier and more satisfied with their relationships than women in same-age relationships.

One famous female who has no qualms about publicly dating younger men is Madonna. Since divorcing Guy Ritchie in 2008, she has dated several men in their twenties and boasted of having lovers three decades younger than her.

One of the reasons younger men date older women in today's society is because they have grown up in a world where women are equals in the workplace, many have worked for female bosses and they are more likely to treat women equally.

Age is just a number and life experiences can be beneficial. Many younger men find older women more grounded, sophisticated and realistic about life, simply because of their life experiences.

Nicole Wipp, a forty-five-year-old attorney and entrepreneur from Detroit, found a perfect match in her husband, Marcus Sutherland, a thirty-three-year-old paramedic. She said she was attracted to a younger man because he was a far cry from the cynical guys closer to her age.

Nicole said, "Younger men don't have the weight of the world on their shoulders, yet." She added, "Older men tend to become cruel over time."

We have used these examples to help you realise that your age can actually become your opportunity for finding happiness, not something that is detrimental to you or holding you back.

It seems that older women-younger men relationships fair far better than older men-younger women relationships. Maybe this is because most of the younger men are single and they are interacting with older women who are already divorced—so they are not entering into a relationship betraying another person or basing it around lies and deceit. On the other hand, single, younger women are often engaging with married men.

Affairs during a partner's pregnancy

Estimates of the number of men who cheat on their partners when they are pregnant are hard to gauge, mainly because pregnancy and childbirth are highly emotional times and make it a very difficult subject to tackle openly.

A 2012 study showed that pregnancy puts partners at a slightly higher risk of infidelity, with an estimated one in ten men cheating on their pregnant partner. We have supported many women who have been cheated on during their pregnancy and witnessed the devastating affect it has on their self-esteem, physical and emotional health.

Some men say they desire as much sex with their pregnant wives/partner, if not more, than they did before pregnancy. So why do they cheat? There are several thoughts as to why men stray during their partner's pregnancy. These range from a lack of sex, to fears about stepping up to the role of being a father. It can also be because they are fearful of hurting the unborn child.

According to Dr Scott Halzman of Brown University Medical School and author of *The Secrets of Happily Married Women* published in 2008, men have a great desire to be needed, loved and cared for. During pregnancy those needs may go unmet. Dr Halzman said, "Sex is a form of emotional closeness; when their partners push them away, they feel rejected, not just sexually, but emotionally."

Sex appears to be the main driver for men to cheat exactly when we need them most. Whether or not this is pure sexual desire or the need for an emotional attachment, or both, only they truly know that. However, without doubt, sex is one of the most important ways for a man to have his need for love and attachment met. Attachment can be defined as a deep and enduring emotional bond that connects one person to another. When their partner is pregnant, a previously healthy sexual relationship may change.

As women, we tend to be more open with friends and family, more prepared to ask for help and share our worries. Men are less likely to do this, so will often turn to a woman who can provide a 'shoulder to cry on' particularly when they feel emotionally rejected.

This can also be why the majority of men who spoke to us said that they were usually the first to say, 'I love you' in a relationship. It is almost as though they say it to secure the love they need from the other person and to maintain the relationship.

In affair scenarios, they may tell the other women they love them to convince them to commit to the relationship on a deeper level. Little does the women realise that this is part of the man's *script*, which says, "I love you, but I am still attached." She only hears "I love you!"

US family counsellor M. Gary Neuman refers to this in his book, *The Truth About Cheating and What you can do to Prevent it*. His results confirmed that the main reason men cheat is emotional. Bearing in mind we have already established that sex and emotions are bound together, his results are hardly surprising.

When asked what led to their cheating, the most common answers given by the men were as follows:

- Forty-eight percent primarily emotional dissatisfaction.
- Thirty-two percent equal emotional and sexual dissatisfaction.
- Eight percent primarily sexual dissatisfaction.

How does this lead to our assertion that men tend to cheat on women when we need them the most?

All the life events and personal storms we discuss in The MAN*Script* demonstrate times when you, as a woman, may have no interest in sex.

For men—being such emotional and physical creatures—this means that for some of them, a lack of sex results in them struggling to keep their feelings alive for their partner and they stray.

Personal storms

Life transitions or personal storms such as pregnancy, the menopause, ill health, juggling careers and domestic chores, caring for elderly relatives, as well as raising children and the empty nest syndrome, can leave women feeling vulnerable, emotional, tired, depressed, sleep deprived and uninterested in sex!

These life challenges can produce a mighty blow to your self-esteem. Then, on top of these issues, to find your partner has cheated on you when you are at your lowest point, can be emotionally crippling. The bullet we referred to earlier as 'annihilating you and ricocheting through your world' can be even harder to deal with in these situations. You will be asking yourself, *How could he do this to me when I need him most?*

In the entanglement between emotion and sex, it is hard for men to separate between the physical act and fulfilment of the emotional need. At times such as pregnancy, giving birth, menopause, or ill health, it is the woman who is in need of emotional support more than ever and it is also a time when she is unlikely to want sex.

It may be fair to say that in such circumstances a man feels rejected. However, he should try to communicate his feelings in a calm manner, which enables the couple to discuss their individual needs, rather than look for comfort outside of the relationship.

Freya, a forty-eight-year-old divorced banker from Yorkshire, told us that an old boyfriend contacted her asking if she would like to meet up. It was said in such a flirtatious manner that she knew exactly what he meant. Without any hesitation, she reminded him that he was married and had just had a new baby. His reply shocked her when he said, "Yes that's right, but she is really busy with the baby right now and I am just in the way."

Needless to say, Freya said, "Thanks, but no thanks."

We cannot stress enough how essential it is to communicate with each other at challenging times in a relationship. However, sometimes the longer we are with someone the less we communicate. How many couples do you see sitting in restaurants hardly talking to each other? How many times have you heard a man or a woman say, "Why didn't he/she talk to me about how they were feeling?"

Talk to your partner, tell him how you are feeling, and listen to what he says.

The impact of these life events is not a constant. They ebb and flow. We have spoken to men who have said they wished they had stayed through the hard times, instead of knee-jerking into seeking self-gratification elsewhere. With hindsight, many men have said that if they were in the same situation again, they would talk to their partner about how they are feeling and that hopefully, it would have brought them closer together, not further apart.

Equally, some men have said that they did try to explain how they were feeling to their partner, but their partner was so focussed on their own issues, they were blind to what they were telling them. Clearly, at times of extreme emotional pressure, this demonstrates how important it is for both partners in a relationship to be aware of the other person's needs.

Mid-life crisis
It is a popular belief that when a marriage or relationship breaks down in mid-life, it is likely to be the man who does the runner. However, it is no surprise to us that more than sixty-five percent of divorces are now instigated by women older than fifty. We are not all doing a 'Shirley Valentine' and

running off to Mykonos, but certainly more of us are taking control of our lives and saying, "Enough!"

Maybe, more fifty-plus women are tiring of their partner's cheating ways and realising that they matter? We also acknowledge that women do cheat on men as well and cause them equally significant pain.

Remember. . .

- Communication maintains the attachment especially at challenging times.
- As much as you talk, never forget to listen.
- There are going to be times in your life when you are uninterested in sex. If you're communicating with your partner they'll hopefully be able to understand this. However, for one in ten men, affairs happen while their partner is pregnant.
- For many men, sex and emotional needs are mixed up together. Some men have admitted that when they are refused sex they can feel emotionally rejected and at this stage seek solace from another woman.
- Embrace and value all your experiences, they have made you who you are. Don't let your age stand in the way of your right to happiness.

"Everything will be OK in the end. If it's not OK, it's not the end."

John Lennon
British singer songwriter, 1940–1980

Chapter Ten

Creating Realistic Expectations

Creating realistic expectations for the future is an important stage of the 'next steps' after an affair. Here, we talk about different potential outcomes after an affair and how to create and work within boundaries that you set for yourself.

If you go to any self-help section in a bookshop, the shelves are full of books asking the question, "Can your marriage be saved?" It doesn't matter what the 'experts' tell you, the only person who truly knows if you want to try to make it work is you. Of course, it takes two people to rebuild a relationship and your partner has a lot to do to make it right. It is also important to ask yourself the question, *"How much of myself am I prepared to lose to stay in this relationship?"*

Don't hang on in a relationship scared to let go if it isn't right for you. Many women tell us how their partners do things they consider to be unforgiveable, but then stay until the next unforgiveable thing happens.

How many unforgiveable things does a man have to do before a woman realises that a relationship she thinks she has or desires is, in reality, not the one she has. If you don't face the truth of a relationship, you are actually living a lie yourself and by living that lie, you are always going to be disappointed.

It is only when you accept that will you have a clearer picture of what you really want to do.

Whether you stay in the relationship or not, it is vital that you have realistic and achievable expectations. If you are to reconcile your relationship your partner also needs to understand this.

He needs to realise all of the following aspects:
- That you will think about his affair a lot.
- That you may have unstable moods.
- He can't expect you to trust again without total transparency over a sustained period of time—up to and after the time you start to feel more secure.
- He needs to be one hundred percent honest about anything you ask him, even if it hurts you.
- He cannot expect you to have sex until you feel ready and he must not make you feel guilty about that.
- He must accept that you will over-analyse situations, even innocent looks or glances, but things will get better over time.
- He cannot say things like 'it is in the past, move on.' It is very real for you and could be, even many years later.

You need to focus on the things you want to achieve, within the limits you have. These are both personal and financial. You must be realistic in the goals that you set, otherwise failing to achieve them is going to tap into possible feelings of 'not being good enough' or 'I am a failure,' both of which you may be feeling already, given the circumstances.

When you can't change the circumstances, change your perspective

A break-up can leave you feeling that you have lost control of your life; immobilised with fear. You cannot control other people's emotions, behaviour, beliefs, or actions. The only things you can control are your own actions, emotions, behaviour and most importantly, your response to him.

Your expectations of that person will have undoubtedly changed. Keeping those expectations 'real' is essential for you to be able to move forward productively. Expecting other people to treat us as we would treat them can lead to such disappointment. You cannot assume anything; to do so is setting yourself up for more hurt. If someone is set in their ways, trying to force them to change will again increase your levels of frustration and irritation.

Setting boundaries is essential to ensuring you are not being impacted on negatively by another person's actions. To set boundaries in a relationship, it is vital that you recognise your own feelings. You have to be able to differentiate yourself from the other person and by that we mean you do not become enmeshed in someone else's thoughts and emotions. You need to create secure boundaries to keep yourself safe so you are not pushed beyond your limits of acceptance of another person's actions.

We fully appreciate how hard this is and often women have told us how they felt so exhausted by it all. It felt easier just to accept what had happened, rather than cause more aggression and upset by raising the subject again. Boundaries are so easily pushed when this happens. This again can make a woman feel worthless and insignificant.

In an affair, the boundary has already been broken. It is not acceptable to have an affair while in another relationship. If you are of a mind to reconcile your relationship, then it is vital that you make your boundaries clearly understood. Sometimes, this can be difficult for your partner to accept, but if he wants the opportunity to right his wrongs, he has to conform.

Remember that your emotions have been traumatised, by setting boundaries you are taking care of yourself. You are making it clear what you will and will not accept and by so doing, you create the groundwork from which your relationship has an opportunity to rebuild.

If you allow your partner to push your boundaries, you run the risk of allowing him to abuse you again. You can also become frustrated and angry with yourself for not being strong enough to stand your ground. Once again, it can feel like your feelings don't matter.

If your partner has left and you are on your own, you still need to create boundaries to protect yourself. Whatever boundaries you set, make sure that you are not tempted to push beyond them. You do not want to feel that somebody has got the better of you.

Working within secure boundaries helps you to know what is appropriate for you and what is not.

Letting go

Rejection is such a powerful emotion and can affect us at the core of who we are; it can affect our identity. When your partner has an affair and leaves, you can feel incredibly rejected and hurt. If you have previously experienced rejection in your life, then these feelings are going to be even more intense.

Along with rejection comes the negative self-talk, 'I am not good enough' or 'I am a failure.' The way to free yourself from these thoughts and feelings is to let go. Yes, we know, it is far easier said than done, but nevertheless, absolutely necessary.

How do you let go? By releasing the expectations that you have and adjusting the assumptions into a more realistic and achievable outcome. You have got to get out of wishful thinking. Wishing achieves nothing, but the possibility of more disappointment. It is time to get your life on track, accept that your life is one hundred percent in the real world and not some fantasy that you are hanging on to.

Try to stay in the moment and take one day at a time. Don't run your thoughts too much ahead into the future; it can be overwhelming. Set small daily goals. Do something for yourself that nurtures you on a daily basis. It may be that you can only rely on yourself to give you the love and care you need right now. All the things you yearn for from that other person—love, care, compassion, compliments—make an effort to give these to yourself, as uncomfortable as this might seem.

Accept that in any moment you are being the best you can be. Acknowledge this with positive affirmation. *"I am doing my best and my best is good enough."* You must believe this.

Staying together

Is it possible to rebuild a relationship after an affair? Many people have written about it, but the first questions should be;

- Can I see myself living with what he has done?
- Will I be constantly wondering who he is talking to or where he is, when I am not with him?

Consider your answers carefully and then take steps to assess your options.

The best relationships involve give and take, but we often find that one partner tends to be the *'giver'* and the other the *'taker'*. To develop a healthy relationship after an affair certain things need to happen. The relationship has to make you both happy. Whatever problems there are in your relationship, these have to be dealt with in such a way that they do not come between you. There will of course be conflict, but you must refrain from the desire to punish each other and work on caring about each other's happiness.

A healthy relationship is healing; love has the capacity to heal the deepest of wounds, but this relies on trust. Trust can only grow between you when you feel able to show your vulnerable side and still be confident that you won't be taken advantage of. This has already been challenged in a huge way by the fact that your partner has had an affair. To heal, you need to feel confident that you are not going to be taken advantage of again, particularly while you express your vulnerable side. You will feel scared of letting your guard down. Your partner really needs to understand this.

You always have choices

When it comes to affairs, some relationships are salvageable, and some are not. It is imperative that you focus on developing yourself. Being desperate and needy can have the opposite effect on the relationship.

Get a clear perspective on your relationship; do not be tempted to see it through rose-tinted glasses. See it for what it really is and his reaction to your hurt may be the key to your decision.

Many women have told us that they felt particularly hurt by their partner's refusal to allow them to ask questions and talk about the Other-Woman. If we express how we feel to our betraying husband/partner, we are often met with anger, which makes us feel even more vulnerable; especially knowing the Other-Woman is probably waiting in the background. Many men actually think of themselves as the 'victim' when they have had to give up the Other-Woman.

Remember, you always have choices, even though they may not be the ones you want. Somewhere in those choices, you have to find the starting point that is going to drive you forward. You know the saying, "No man is an island." No woman is either. Be brave enough to ask for help when you need it. Never think you have to hide in shame.

Seek out people who have an empathic and positive attitude and who will support you. Choose an environment that is conducive to your wellbeing and recovery. Try really hard not to get stuck in the past. You have the power to change things if you really want to.

Be mindful though, the majority of women are naturally carers and as such, we can be taken advantage of. Many of us work in caring, compassionate roles, tuned to give, rather than to receive. It is this type of personality that starts to feel sorry for the partner who has cheated.

Julia, co-author of The MAN*Script*, said, "I am naturally a caring person and I know that no matter how angry I was with my husband, somehow I felt sorry for him, because I could see what a mess he was making of his life."

Often, feeling this way causes a conflict within us and we start to feel more let down, which in turn exacerbates the anger. It isn't always good to be a giver, when you are on the receiving end of such betrayal.

Remember. . .

- Your emotions have been traumatised; by setting secure boundaries to work within, you are taking care of yourself.
- Surround yourself with supportive people.
- If you're a naturally caring person you can find yourself feeling sorry for your partner, even offering support and guidance to him during troubled times.
- Certain things need to happen to develop a healthy relationship after an affair. The relationship has to make you both happy. Whatever problems there are in your relationship, these have to be dealt with in such a way that they do not come between you. There will of course be conflict, but you must refrain from the desire to punish each other and work on caring about each other's happiness.
- A healthy relationship is one that heals.

"True reconciliation does not consist in merely forgetting the past."

Nelson Mandela,
South African anti-apartheid politician and philanthropist,
President of South Africa 1994–1999

Chapter Eleven

The Reconciliation Script
The Rules You Set And He Must Follow

We have been told that this is one of the most important chapters in the book by our early readers. This is the Reconciliation *Script* and outlines what he must do if he wants you to give him another chance. Love is not just a word, it has to be an action too.

Essential steps to healing a relationship after an affair

The first thing we must re-emphasise is that his affair was not about you or anything you did. It was about him putting his needs ahead of your relationship. If he wants to keep you, you have to set the rules and make it clear to him that these rules are cast in stone.

A partner who is genuinely sorry will show remorse and be willing to bend over backwards, forwards, in fact any way it takes, to be given the chance of reconciliation. This is such an important point to emphasise: it is the action he takes to prove his remorse that will help convince you of his true feelings towards repairing your relationship. What he does is more important than what he says.

The evidence will be written on his face, in the words he

uses and in the actions he takes. You know him better than anyone; trust your gut instinct.

A genuinely remorseful partner is going to feel guilt and it is very tempting for the betrayed partner to want this guilt to last a very long time. In fairness, if the partner is doing everything he can for a sustained period of time to reconcile the relationship then the guilt must be allowed to be put to bed. Together, it is helpful if you come to a point of acceptance. You can work through his guilt together and this will help you to start to feel close to him again, providing he is genuine in his guilt.

However, if he cannot acknowledge the reality of his actions it is unlikely that he will change the way he behaves. You cannot change what you don't acknowledge. We would encourage you to stay strong to ensure he realises what he needs to do. We have found that many men want a quick fix. They want you to forget about it and pretend it never happened. Not only is this virtually impossible, but if you let him get away with that, he has no reason to think he cannot do it again and you will accept it.

If he is wallowing in self-pity regarding the Other-Woman and telling you he needs to let go slowly, forget it! We understand that the feelings are going to take time to re-adjust to reality, but what is unacceptable is that he hangs on to that previous relationship in the hope that his feelings will fade. The truth about such a scenario is he is hedging his bets, just in case the reconciliation with you doesn't work.

One of the women we have worked with is social worker Louise, thirty-five from London, who told us how her husband kept telling her, "Just give me a hint that you will take me back and we can be normal again. I can never accept there will be no us, but I am scared to have no-one and be alone."

The reality is that Louise's husband was a coward, not prepared to give up the Other-Woman until he had guarantees from the wife he had betrayed that everything would be normal again! This is emotional cruelty and as Louise said, "He played with my mind in such a cruel way, I was on my knees and he wanted me to be the one to carry on as normal. It felt like he was emotionally battering me."

You cannot and should not have to deal with how much he misses the Other-Woman, or how scared he is of being alone. You have given him a chance. It is up to him to respect you and make all the effort. He is being totally selfish if he thinks you can tolerate him slowly withdrawing from the Other-Woman, who, let's not forget, colluded in ripping your world apart.

He may have criticised you as part of his *script* for not having enough sex with him, for being moody, gaining weight or not looking as attractive as you once did in his eyes. Who knows what excuses he will come up with? Only you know how it feels to be on the receiving end of comments like these. It is your partner's responsibility to help you re-establish your self-worth and self-esteem.

We acknowledge that it can be hard for the man, but maybe for the first time in his life, he has to accept that everything has to be one hundred percent transparent. That includes all his bank account information, his passwords, mobile telephone details and anything else that you feel the need to be privy to. The need for openness can be a trigger for the man to feel a total invasion of his privacy. If he can accept that this is part of the healing process for you both, then hopefully he can provide this information if required in a tolerant and understanding manner. Let's be clear and fair here, trust has to be re-earned.

In the beginning of the reconciliation process it has to be understood by your partner that there is no trust. However, for a sustained period of time and with one hundred percent transparency and honesty, that trust can start to be regained. You cannot check up on him forever and yes, there will probably always be an element of suspicion, but providing he handles those suspicious moments in a loving and caring manner, then your fears will be unfounded. Again, trust your gut instinct.

Ten rules for reconciliation

If a man wants to stay with his wife/partner after betraying her, these are the rules he must follow:

1. Absolutely no contact with the Other-Woman; no messages, no telephone call, no texts, no email, nothing. Basically, no contact between your partner and his former lover, whatsoever!

2. That other person must not exist anymore. He must remove the Other-Woman. If he is serious about rebuilding your relationship, he will do this. If he can't or refuses, you have to ask yourself why you are trying, when he clearly doesn't care enough.

3. Your partner has to permit you to distrust him. If he gets angry with you every time you question him, he doesn't appreciate the impact of his affair on you and the fact that you can't trust him right now. He must accept that you will be carrying a burden of distrust and by staying with him you are making yourself vulnerable to hurt again.

4. If he gets angry that it is taking too long for you to trust him, tell him, "It is rather that you are taking too long to prove to me that you are worthy of my trust again."

5. Actions speak louder than words. It is an old cliché, but it is true. Rebuilding your relationship is up to him and if he wants to regain your trust, he has to make sure that his actions make you feel appreciated, loved and that you have his full attention.

6. The person who has had the affair has to be the one to help heal their partner. Above all, not only do they have to say how sorry they are, but they need to show the hurt person that they really mean it.

7. The person who has had the affair has to be totally transparent going forward.

8. The cheater has to talk about the issue(s) that led to him choosing to have an affair. He has no right to get angry when you question him.

9. You have to rebuild trust. This can only be achieved during a sustained period of time and requires patience, understanding and total honesty.

10. Forgiveness needs to be earned. Forgiveness is a choice and it doesn't come easily. Forgiveness is not about forgetting or condoning. It is about accepting that no one is perfect and mistakes are made. If your partner is truly sorry for his actions and does everything he can to help you heal, then forgiveness can be achieved, if you so choose. It is forgiveness that releases the anger and heals the hurt you feel, in other words, it's about setting yourself free.

It's important to acknowledge that being able to forgive is no easy task; we know that, but even if you can't reconcile your relationship there will come a time when not being able to forgive will prevent you from moving on with your life.

Remember forgiveness does not mean condoning what your partner did, it means setting yourself free from the burden.

When we first met stay at home mum Maisie, thirty-seven, from Nottingham, she told us that she would never ever forgive her husband for having an affair. They had divorced ten years previously, but she still hated him for what he did. We met up with her again a year later and she told us how actually being able to sum up the courage to contact him and say, "I forgive you", had a profound impact on her and she felt a massive sense of relief.

Suddenly, she wasn't carrying his baggage around any longer or imagining him with the Other-Woman, she was at last free.

Don't trawl your mind

Probably like every woman who has been betrayed, we have to acknowledge the pictures you have in your head and they can be really difficult to erase. The more you want to know about the physical act, the more you have to recognise that you are torturing yourself with the images that you see in your mind. We strongly recommend that you try to not do this. We know that these pictures in your head will never go away completely, but this is something you have to accept. When you can accept the images in your mind you will be able to let them go more easily; fighting them will only make them persist.

Acknowledge the setbacks

It is really important to understand that almost always there will be setbacks in the reconciliation process. If you accept that these are a part of re-establishing the boundaries in which your relationship is now functioning, then you will get through these setbacks and come out the other side on a more solid footing.

You have to think carefully about what you can and cannot live with, making empty threats to control your partner's response is not the way to go about making you feel better. It has to be said that regardless of how much effort your partner may make in helping you heal the hurt and rebuild the trust, if you can't get over his affair, then the kindest thing for both of you is to accept that and walk away.

If he uses setbacks as a reason to return to the Other-Woman, forget trying to reconcile your relationship because it is highly likely he had never given up on her in the first place.

Clarissa, a thirty-seven-year-old woman, from Ireland, told us, "I kept finding messages on my husband's telephone from the Other-Woman. Every time I confronted him we argued and once he was so aggressive towards me that I told him to leave. He went back to her and he said it was my fault and that I had pushed him to do it because I threw him out! It made me doubt my sanity and once again he made himself the victim."

Clarissa's husband made himself out to be the victim, which was part of his defence *script*, while trying to blame Clarissa and make her out to be the guilty partner. None of this is true and if your partner does the same to you, do not accept the blame.

At some point, if you want this relationship to work and possibly be better than it ever has been, you are going to have to make a decision to cross the biggest barrier yet and that is to have sex with him. This is when those images in your head can make that barrier feel a hundred feet high and fifty feet deep.

Resuming a sexual relationship

This is possibly the toughest obstacle to get over after an affair. The pictures of your partner and the Other-Woman having sex are, at first, impossible to erase from your mind. This makes having sex really difficult, if not impossible, to begin with. You need to build up the intimacy slowly with your partner, responding appropriately to your feelings. Expect the tears to flow. Your partner needs to make you feel special, loved and adored, for a long time to come. Maybe forever, you will need reassurance that you and you alone, are the most important, cherished person in his life.

Patience

If you are going to build your relationship, you need to give it as much time as is necessary. Often the partner who has had an affair wants to rebuild it as soon as possible. This can lead to conflict and he must understand that there is no quick fix to the aftermath of an affair. He is either prepared to accept this or not and therefore, patience is vital. He must understand and give you space.

There is no time limit as to how long it takes to heal after an affair; every partnership is different. Some heal more quickly than others. This is very much down to the personalities of those involved and how well they communicate and understand each other's needs. It is also about how much they both want to repair and make the relationship work and how much respect, care and love they have for each other.

Affairs can make or break a partnership. Many couples that have experienced betrayal have gone on to have an even better relationship than they had before the affair. The understanding of what each other wants is improved and more effort has been put into maintaining a healthy sex life and better communication.

Grief is about loss, and loss is about what you do not have any longer. That can mean many things and not just the end of a relationship. It can mean staying with your partner, but feeling the loss of trust, security, love, respect, confidence, honesty. All of these losses need to be processed before you can let go and move forward. We cover the process of grief in Chapter Twelve.

Remember. . .
- The person who has had the affair has to be the one to help their partner heal.
- You cannot change what you don't acknowledge.
- Forgiveness sets you free, it doesn't mean you condone what your partner has done.
- Love needs actions, it's not just a word.
- If the reassurance you need is given to you regularly, over a period of time, there comes a point when you will feel you are thinking and talking about the affair less.

"You can never cross the ocean unless you have the courage to lose sight of the shore."

Sir Christopher Columbus,
Italian explorer, 1451-1506

Chapter Twelve

When Staying Together Is Not An Option

What happens when staying together is not an option? There are various stages of grieving when a relationship has ended, and we will talk you through that process now so you are not alone.

Not everyone wants, or is able to, save a relationship after infidelity. It may also be that you have no choice when your partner decides to leave you for the Other-Woman.

The decision to end the relationship may be yours, but it is not something you had planned to happen in your life. We have described what a cheating man needs to do to rebuild trust, but sometimes even that is not enough to heal the deep pain of betrayal.

When we are faced with the end of a relationship, whether we want it or not, fear grips us all. Whether you stay or it ends, you need to show yourself some self-compassion. After all, your partner didn't show you compassion when he cheated on you. It is time to recognise your self-worth and look after your physical and emotional wellbeing.

We don't all have a light bulb moment, for some of us there is confusion, a fog in our minds for many years, making it impossible to think clearly.

How to make the decision

There are several important questions you may need to consider before making your decision.

- What will happen to the children, how will they react or cope?
- What about my financial security?
- How will I cope on my own?
- Am I strong enough to deal with a divorce?
- How will our friends and family react?
- Can I live on my own?
- Can I ever see myself in a new relationship?

We probably all know women who have stayed in a marriage or relationship because of their children or financial dependence on their partner. Some of those women may tell you that if they had their time again, they would have left much earlier.

For some women, facing life alone can feel very frightening. It can also bring positive self-fulfilment and huge rewards. You probably won't be able to see that far ahead when you are going through it, but one day you will look back and realise how much stronger you have become and what you have achieved.

Some people believe that it is not the infidelity that delivers the fatal blow to a relationship, but rather the way the infidelity is dealt with after the affair. In particular, how the cheating man deals with what he has done can make or break the relationship. If he continually justifies his actions and flippantly tells you, "Well it's finished, so move on," the chances are that he is not going to change.

Thirty-three-year-old Caroline, a mother of two children,

from Barcelona, told us how she chose to stay with her husband after she discovered his infidelity.

"I made the decision because of my children. My husband was part of a group of work colleagues who met for lunch every couple of months. The woman he had the affair with attended the lunches. Years later my husband was still meeting with the same colleagues every six months or so, even though some of them had changed jobs. Every time my husband attended one of the lunches it made me think about his affair and I always asked him if she was going. He would always answer sharply and was clearly irritated by my questioning and suspicion. Five years after his affair, I asked if she was going, to which he replied, "Why are you being like this?""

Caroline had spent five years secretly trying to deal with his affair, she had asked a reasonable question and yet he turned it around, leaving her feeling guilty for asking. Caroline said it was then that she realised nothing had changed, he was simply taking her for granted.

Pauline, a thirty-eight-year-old journalist from Cardiff, told us, "I kept going for my children and pretended I was happy. We went on a family holiday, which had already been booked before I discovered my husband's affair. Although it didn't leave my mind for a second, I kept a smiling face to the outside world, mainly for the sake of my children. When we came back home to reality, I crumbled, it was just all too much to cope with."

When Pauline told her husband how she was feeling, his response was, "We have just had a nice holiday, you really need to let it go, because it's in the past now. I thought you were OK about it because we had such a lovely time."

As she said to us, "It wasn't in the past for me, it was as real as the day my suspicions had first been confirmed, but he was flippantly dismissing my feelings and expected it to be business as usual. That was my light bulb moment. I saw quite clearly then that he didn't care enough or value how I felt. It was staring me in the face, he was never going to change and I was not going to be allowed to talk about it. I couldn't live like that."

What happens if the denial continues

In the case of co-author of The MAN*Script*, Julia, her husband continually protested his innocence and bombarded her with declarations of love and a desire to save her marriage. He did this while continuing his relationship with the Other-Woman. His constant denial, when there was categorical evidence that he was continuing with his affair, was very traumatic and cruel. At times, it sent Julia into a downward spiral, leaving her feeling psychologically battered and bruised.

The pain cannot begin to heal when your partner is still involved with someone else. Nor can a healthy return to a marriage begin. Yes, he has been caught out and says he is sorry and he wants to make it work with you. However, his feelings for the Other-Woman may keep him from fully committing to that process. This is because somewhere within him, he still needs the Other-Woman.

If he hasn't already broken it off with her, he may be willing to do so for the sake of his marriage, but he might also feel sad until he really gets 'over her.' If he remains in the least bit involved with the Other-Woman, even if it is just a telephone call, then the affair isn't finished. Therefore, any reconciliation under these circumstances isn't possible. The 'halfway house' scenario preferred by many men just does not work and is downright cruel.

Some men justify their actions after they have been caught out, by telling people that their wife or partner has made it clear they don't want to be with them. What these men seem incapable of realising is that the betrayed partner is unlikely to even contemplate rekindling their relationship, unless the Other-Woman is totally and utterly off the scene.

This appears to be quite common in 'mid-life crisis' affairs. It is the fear of getting old that drives men to have affairs—often with younger women, which in turn leads to them having a fear of being alone at that time in their lives. Many seem incapable of letting go of the Other-Woman, in case their partner doesn't want them back.

Many women told us that after their partner's infidelity had been discovered, their husband or partner asked them the question, "What do you want me to do to prove I want to be with you?"

If he doesn't understand how hurt you are by his actions, that his actions demonstrate a lack of 'wanting to be with you', then he is probably not making the effort he should be, or indeed the effort you deserve.

Whether you have made the choice to end the relationship or your partner has left you for the Other-Woman, the most powerful thing you can do is to take away from him the control he has on your life. Put yourself in the driving seat.

If your partner has decided to leave you, it may help you to focus on all the bad points about him. You really have to do this to maintain your strength. You literally have to keep thinking about the bad things, repetitively. The accumulative effect of these bad memories will help reinforce to you that you can be OK without him. Focusing on the negative helps to break the attachment. You may not want to do this initially, but if you are being presented with the end of your relationship, this exercise really does help.

The grieving process when a relationship has ended

The end of a relationship is a devastating experience. It is really hard to accept when it's finished. It is so painful that you avoid the need to grieve at all costs, hoping that the relationship can be salvaged. However, at some point the grief process has to begin, otherwise you are going to remain stuck and unable to move on with your life.

Going through the grief process is extremely painful, but unless you go through it you won't find happiness when you come out the other side. Don't make any rash, life-changing decisions while grieving. We know women who threw their husbands out, sold up and moved to another part of the country, only to regret what they had done later down the line.

We have also spoken to women who have had some impulsive sexual encounters with men after they discovered their husband's affair. Don't go out of the frying pan into the fire. Make decisions when you are in the right frame of mind. Don't lose sight of who you really are. Your self-esteem is your responsibility, never give it to someone else.

You may feel utterly overwhelmed, immobilised and haunted by loss, fear and despair, facing life without you partner. Be kind to yourself, allow yourself to grieve and go through the stages of grief and letting go.

The need to know why

Sometimes there is a desperate need to understand why the relationship has ended. It will be all you can think about. Some people will turn to friends and family, but others will find it too embarrassing and will be carrying the false burden of shame and failure.

One minute you will have acceptance and say to yourself, '*Of course, it's finished*' and the next minute you are back to the never-ending cycle of non-acceptance. On a daily basis, it may feel like you rediscover the loss because repetitively you don't want to believe it has happened.

Denial

The impact of betrayal can be so strong that it's hard to accept it's actually happened.

Have you heard yourself say these words? "I can't believe this is happening, this can't be true, I can't live without him."

Your relationship has been everything to you, your world and your life, so is it any wonder you cannot accept it is finished? After all, this is the person you thought you knew and you would never have believed he could do this to you.

"*If I had a penny for every time a woman sat in front of me and said, I cannot believe what he has done—I thought I knew him—I'd be very wealthy.*" P. Hollings, divorce lawyer.

The grieving process cannot begin until you face the fact that the relationship cannot be salvaged. It is only when you accept this that you will be able to start to let go.

I can make this right

The thought of being without your partner is so intolerable

that you might go into overdrive, thinking about ways to win him back. You convince yourself that if you make yourself more attractive, attentive and sexy, he will not be able to resist rekindling your relationship. This is really dangerous ground for your emotional wellbeing because you are accepting responsibility for the reasons why he had an affair.

You will cling to any hope that seems possible, which prevents you from acknowledging the loss of someone you love. Bearing in mind all the emotions that are present during this phase, it makes it almost impossible to see things with clarity and reality.

As much as you think that taking responsibility for his affair will somehow mend your relationship; it won't. All it will do in the long term is make you feel that whatever you do is not good enough; you believe it is your fault and you could have put it right.

Prolonging the process of letting go

If your partner has left and you are of a mind to try and persuade him to come back and give it another go, you may be only temporarily relieving the pain if he ends up walking out on you again. We feel you are putting yourself in a vulnerable position, being led by the feelings of love and loss.

You need to think about this, really, really carefully and ask yourself the question; "Are you prepared to go through the hurt and pain of breaking up and trying reconciling more than once, before you know for certain it is time to let go?"

Dealing with the anger

Feeling angry is acknowledging that you matter and that you

do not deserve to be disrespected and treated in this way. Anger is a motivating emotion. It is full of energy, which helps to keep you going in the initial stages. This largely depends on the type of person you are, your temperament and your ability to express anger.

Some people do not express their anger easily, preferring to internalise their emotions, which can lead to them becoming depressed and unable to see a way out of their pain. Anger, whether directed at your partner or yourself, is a part of the grieving process and a sign that you are working through your loss.

Begin to accept
You may get to the stage where you accept your relationship is finished, because you have to, not because you want to. You are beginning to realise that no matter what you say or do, it is the end. You need to create boundaries that you feel comfortable with and that are acceptable to you. This particularly matters when there are children involved.

Hope for the future
As you give up the hope of trying to save a failing relationship, your actions and feelings must be directed at the belief that you can have a successful and happy life without your ex. This might not be easy to accept, but once you do, it can open you up to opportunities that you may never have thought possible.

Accept the process
It is helpful for you to understand that the grieving process is unstable; your emotions may be erratic for years to come.

Do not be worried about this. It is a normal part of suffering loss. It is well documented that suffering brings about the most growth potential within an individual. It is how you deal with it that will determine the outcome.

It is important to emphasise that you will experience many setbacks. The grieving process following betrayal is going to be full of ups and downs. Some downs will push you back so far you will feel as though you can never recover.

Olivia, a fifty-nine-year-old coffee shop owner from Brazil, told us how she thought she had come to terms with her husband's affair, but many years later and completely out of the blue, she went crashing back down.

"I can't explain why, but I realised I had never got over it, I was simply functioning."

There is no hard and fast rule about this process because grieving is a very individual response. There may be days when it feels like you are going through all the stages in one go, or certain parts of the grieving process are reignited, and you can feel knocked back. Please understand that this is normal after all you have been through.

The impact of grief can be so debilitating that you may try various ways to avoid it. The hurt is so intense that if you can find ways of delaying it, you will. However, the reality is that the longer you delay facing the truth and feelings of grief, the harder it gets. You have to be prepared to go through it, not around it, over it or under it, but face it head on. When you can accept this, you are on the road to healing and recovery.

To help you understand this process, we have written a list of losses that you may find yourself grieving for:

- I am grieving the loss of the relationship I had.
- I am grieving the loss of the man who is not who I thought he was.
- I am grieving the loss of the trust I had in him.
- I am grieving the loss of the belief that he would be faithful to me.
- I am grieving the loss of the security he gave me.
- I am grieving the loss of my identity in the relationship.
- I am grieving the loss of the role I played in the relationship with my partner.
- I am grieving the loss of the life I had.
- I am grieving the loss of the man I thought I knew, in the knowledge that I can never get him back.
- I am grieving the loss of the future I thought I would have with him.

There is a lot of grieving that has to be done before you can truly let go of the pain. It is understandable that you may well believe that you will never recover the loss of your relationship. We know and understand just how intense that pain can be.

However, if you approach the grieving process with kindness to yourself, ensuring that you make yourself the priority in every area of your life, you will get stronger and you will come through this.

You may want to write a letter to your partner expressing all the thoughts and emotions you feel. However, the one thing you shouldn't do, is send it to him! Take the letter, put it in a flameproof pot, get a lighter, make sure it is safe and set the letter on fire. Watch it burn and as you do so, breathe away all the emotions and thoughts you have just poured onto that piece of paper. Let them go. Do this exercise as many times as it takes to clear your heart and mind.

Remember. . .

- Your self-esteem belongs to you, never give the responsibility for it to anyone else.
- Being without your partner, however frightening, can also bring positive self-fulfilment and unexpected rewards.
- Losing a partner after an affair is a grieving process that can take time.
- You may be able to prolong the grieving process—and the acceptance/letting go—but it will catch up with you eventually, potentially even decades later.
- Show kindness to yourself—it will get better.

"In the middle of difficulty lies opportunity."

Albert Einstein,
German physicist, 1879–1955

Chapter Thirteen

Moving On

In this chapter, we help you to move forward by looking after yourself, stop obsessing about 'them' and build up your strength, confidence and identity again.

Whatever decision you make, it is your decision. Friends and family should support you in that choice. If it has ended because you wanted it to, or because he has left you with no choice, you must understand that you have done nothing wrong. We know women who ended their relationship after their partner's affair, only to get the blame from people around them for the break up.

This is often the time that some men become very difficult about financial support. It may be the only way he can exert control over you and make you panic, thinking you need him. He may be under the influence of the Other-Woman, who is determined that he won't be spending his money on you, instead of her.

You also need to be aware of the character traits of your partner that you may have found difficult to deal with in your relationship, which are likely to be reinforced through separation or divorce. For example, if your partner was controlling or self-centred, those behaviours are likely to come into play through the separation process. If you haven't before, this is when you really need to seek legal advice.

It is about you now

It is hard to practice self-compassion and take control of your life when you are being emotionally pulled in so many directions. However, it is time to get out from under your duvet. By now you have watched the full collection of *Bridget Jones* and eaten tons of ice cream! Show yourself some self-compassion. Do whatever it takes to boost your self-confidence and to start to feel good about yourself.

Whether you want to win him back from the Other-Woman, never want anything to do with him again or have decided to stay with him, he needs to feel the fear you have been feeling. He will see you go from being the needy and neurotic wife or partner, to a confident, self-assured woman. The chances are that when he sees this transformation, he will be desperate to get you back. After all, he never intended to lose you in the first place.

Remember the scene in the film, *Pretty Woman*, when Julia Roberts dressed in designer clothes, carrying bags and bags of branded items, goes back to the shop that had previously refused to serve her. She stares at them straight in the face and says, "Big mistake. Big. Huge!"

Once he sees the transformation in you, he could shift the blame for his life of woe to the Other-Woman. She will be on the receiving end of his dissatisfaction, instead of you. If he starts to pay her less attention and focus on you, she is likely to become the needy, clingy one who irritates him. Lock away your bunnies because this is the time the Other-Woman may come knocking on your door to tell you all the grizzly details of their affair.

Initially, starting to take care of yourself could be as simple as going for walks or coffee with friends you have been avoiding for fear of awkward conversations. It may be a new hairstyle, new clothes or makeup. Do whatever it takes to start you on the road to recovery, and feeling confident and happy again.

For some women who have never been without a boyfriend or husband, this can be a scary, but enlightening time.

Managing your anger

Lorena Bobbitt gained worldwide fame in 1993, when she cut off the penis of her husband with a carving knife while he was asleep. After chopping it off, she took it in her car and threw it into a field! She was later found 'not guilty' due to insanity, caused by the history of abuse she had endured throughout their relationship. Her experiences were seen to be the cause of her having an irresistible impulse to sexually wound him.

Lady Sarah Graham-Moon didn't go as far as Lorena Bobbitt, but she cut off the arms of her unfaithful husband's Saville Row suits. She then hurled paint over his prized BMW car and left seventy bottles of his vintage champagne on the doorsteps of all her neighbours.

Another famous scissor-wielding woman was Pamela Bordes, who had a high-profile relationship with the newspaper editor Andrew Neil. When he dumped her, she cut the crotch out of all his trousers.

Many of us would love to see our unfaithful partners suffer, but we don't need to do a Lorena Bobbitt, a Sarah Graham-Moon or a Pamela Bordes. All these women and many more who have taken revenge in a moment of anger—which we have all felt—are likely to have later regretted their actions.

Remember, when you are going through the grieving process, don't make any rash decisions, especially those driven by anger. Revenge is best served chilled and the best revenge of all is to live your life for you and become a strong, happy, self-fulfilled woman without him. Believe us, it will drive him insane.

As Ivana Trump said when faced with Donald Trump's unfaithfulness, "Don't get mad, get everything."

To her, everything may have been financial or material gain, but everything should be about being true to you. Of course, you will feel immense anger but use your anger to drive yourself forward instead of wasting it on a man who betrayed you.

Hate that lies within is just waiting to be triggered. It can lead you to express anger to the wrong people at the wrong time. Remember, sitting with hate in your heart does not help you move to a happier place. It is more beneficial for you to let it go and be free. Hate will only serve to trap you in the past.

How to stop obsessing about 'them'

What you must do to enable yourself to move on, whether you stay with your partner or not, is to stop the overwhelming obsession to think about him and the Other-Woman as a couple. The more you focus on what they have done or are doing, the more power and influence you are giving them in your life.

It would be unrealistic to tell you to stop thinking about your partner and the Other-Woman together; that simply is not possible without practice and help. You have probably thought of nothing but him and her together for days, weeks, months, even years. They have been the last thing you think of at night and the first thing you think of when you wake.

You can be having a perfectly good day and all of a sudden, thoughts of your partner with her will come into your mind and the day is ruined because you can't think of anything else. This is why it is absolutely essential that you learn how to stop the destructive cycle. Your thoughts are not the same as reality. You have to force yourself to redirect your thoughts into building your self-esteem. It can help to have a pen and paper handy and in that moment of turmoil write down your thoughts.

We recommend you list all the positive and good things:
- You like about yourself.
- You have achieved.
- That people have said about you.
- That you are capable of.
- How you have helped other people.

Some women over exaggerate the qualities they perceive the Other-Woman may have, whilst underestimating their own qualities and value. Depending on your own insecurities and self-worth, you may or may not have a tendency to build the Other-Woman up to a disproportionate level of who they really are. The truth is that what she is like is totally irrelevant to you. Let's not forget, this woman got involved with a man who was already in a relationship and that speaks volumes.

The next thing you have to do is to take action. You have to do everything you can to distract yourself away from these thoughts. You need to do something that is beneficial to you. For example, take some exercise or do whatever it takes to make yourself feel and look good. You really have to get to like yourself again.

The thoughts and images of your partner and the Other-Woman will not go away overnight and you have to accept it will take time. The suggestions we make below are designed to get you started on the process of letting go of these thoughts. Remember, this woman has either taken, or has tried to take, your partner away from you. Why would you let her now take away your self-esteem and your right to internal happiness? No one is worth that. The scenario you play out in your mind could be the projection of the relationship you want for yourself.

How to change the horror film in your mind

The pictures you have in your head of your partner and the Other-Woman are like the two main characters in the worst horror film you ever watched. The images you see appear to have a life of their own.

You may imagine your partner and the Other-Woman:
- Having wild passionate sex.
- Being loving towards each other.
- Never having a cross word.
- Having a wonderful life.
- Being consumed with each other.
- Sending each other passionate text messages.
- Loving each other more than the two of you did.
- Never showing anger, frustration, irritation to each other.

- Him suddenly becoming this perfect person and her getting all the benefits.
- His family and your friends thinking she is wonderful.
- The two of them laughing at you.

There are probably many more thoughts, which are specific to your own experiences, but these seem to be the most common according to the women we have helped and spoken with.

Take a moment to consider these points carefully. Surely you can see that this perfect relationship in your head is more of a fantasy than will ever be a reality?

It doesn't matter what time of the day or night it is, the horror film never seems to end. Now, think of this. You wrote the *script* for this horror film. You directed the characters, you made them play out the worst scenarios possible, the ones that punish you on a daily basis. Only you, as the director of your thoughts have the ability to change the *script*. You can make the characters do anything you want them to do. It is time for you to remember all the difficult things about his personality.

Remember all the times he didn't step up to the mark, all the times you were left wanting. Was your relationship all that it seemed? Imagine him behaving like he used to with you but towards the Other-Woman. You know him well. You have the ability to rewrite the *script* according to what makes you happy. If you repeat this exercise several times, you will disempower the images that invade your head.

Each time you obsess about the relationship between your partner and the Other-Woman, you disconnect from yourself and by disconnecting from yourself, you are never going to be able to live a fulfilling life that is right for you. Your obsession decreases your ability to be open to new opportunities that may come your way.

Keep telling yourself:
- I matter.
- My life is important.
- I deserve respect.
- Only I can make myself happy.
- I am unique.

Here is another helpful exercise to help you with your obsessive thoughts. Initially, we want you to allow him and the Other-Woman ten minutes of every hour. In the ten minutes (time yourself) you will need to totally saturate your mind, thinking about nothing but them. Really feel your thoughts, your worry and your anger towards them.

After that, for the next fifty minutes only think about you and what you need to do to make yourself happy and strong again. If during this time, thoughts of them come back into your head, take action and distract yourself.

A good way to stop yourself thinking about them during your time is to wear an elastic band on your wrist. Each time they come into your head, ping the band. You may have a sore wrist, but it will be worth it, as it will help you redirect your thoughts towards yourself in a positive way. One day, you will suddenly realise that you haven't thought about them for a while. They have become insignificant to you and you feel indifferent about them. That is a very good place for you to be.

Remember. . .
- Only you, as the director of your thoughts, have the ability to change the *script*.
- The horror film you play out in your head is not based in reality. You know your partner and what he's like. He won't be able to keep up the pretence with the Other-Woman forever.
- Force yourself not to think about them for at least part of your waking hours.
- Write a list of all the things you know are good and positive and true about yourself.
- To move on you need to keep looking forward.

"To conquer fear is the beginning of wisdom."

Bertrand Russell,
British philosopher, mathematician and historian, 1872–1970

Chapter Fourteen

Time to Shine

Here we offer four steps to help *you* to embrace *you* in *your entirety*. If you have been using the My Freedom Diary and writing down your thoughts and feelings to help you get over the affair, now is the time to look back and reflect upon how far you have come.

Step One: Embrace your fears

By embracing your fears, you have the perfect antidote to accepting your new life. Whether you remain with your partner or not, your relationship has changed forever. How you go forward will be determined by the relationship you have with yourself and the value you give that relationship.

We encourage you to be brave enough to face up to your fears. We fully appreciate there may be many fears in your current situation. We have yet to meet a person who does not have any anxieties, so trust us when we say you are not alone.

In the following list, we have changed the word *fear* to the word *embrace* so that you can feel what it is like when you change your perspective.

Don't rush through them but take the time to feel each statement as you read each one out loud:

- I embrace being alone.
- I embrace the unknown.
- I embrace change.
- I embrace starting again.
- I embrace that it will take time to be able to trust again.
- I embrace that I have the strength to cope.
- I embrace the lifestyle I will have.
- I embrace my children.
- I embrace my social life.
- I embrace my identity.
- I embrace being attractive to somebody else.
- I embrace being wanted.
- I embrace being loved.
- I embrace my worthiness.
- I embrace being happy again.
- I embrace the challenge of finding happiness, in whatever form that may take.

We hope this book has helped you understand the various MAN*Scripts* men use when being unfaithful and has shown you how to deal with the fallout and aftermath when faced with being betrayed.

As much as you were one part of a partnership, you are one whole of a person in your own right.

You must remember that it takes a man with certain character traits to be able to cheat and lie. Never forget it was *his* choice to have an affair. Never let it be said you made him have an affair and it was your fault.

If a relationship hurts, it is a relationship in which

something is wrong. Rather than look for an answer outside the relationship, men need to take the time to talk and improve communication with their partner.

Step Two: Take back control of your life

If your partner has left you, don't let yourself live his life. The more you obsess about his life with the other woman, the more you allow yourself to be controlled by him. In all of his deceit and lies you have been manipulated. You have unknowingly been playing a supporting role in his double life.

You need to take the control back and start to look after yourself. Now concentrate on your life. Make a point of doing something every day which nurtures you. Make yourself count.

Never beat yourself up with internal self-doubt and recrimination. You have suffered enough, don't suffer more pain by telling yourself you are not good enough or the Other-Woman is better than you. She certainly is not.

Remember that no one can make you do anything and no one can make you believe anything unless you allow them to. When you feel trapped by fear, you are losing the grip on the keys to unlock your freedom and future happiness. You can do it.

Step Three: Detach from your partner

We would like to share with you this unique exercise that has helped many women.

Imagine you are interviewing men to be your life partner. In through the door walks the man who has betrayed you. He sits down in front of you and you assess him for the job. You ask him to describe himself.

He replies, "I am a liar, duplicitous and a cheat. I am manipulative, controlling and blame other people for my actions and decisions I make. I can be kind, caring and very loving, but only if it benefits me. I like the attention of other women and feel good about myself when they flatter me. I get the attention I deserve, even if I hurt other people in the process."

You listen carefully, and with strength and determination you tell him, "The job states that I am looking for someone who is loyal, honest, trustworthy and loving. You don't meet the criteria I'm looking for. You haven't got the job."

Step Four: Accept your new life

Many of the women we spoke to use the word 'cursed' when referring to how they feel after being cheated on. It's natural after a bad experience to feel that you are the victim of a bad karma.

In fact, rather than a curse, you have been given a new chance, an opportunity to change your life. You have been afforded the insight to know what is right for you and more importantly, what is not right. Use every aspect of what you have learned through this experience to bring the good back into your life.

Never let your future be controlled by what you have lost, but rather embrace the opportunity you have been given to make a better future for yourself. We promise that one day you will look back and realise how much better your life is, how much stronger you are and how much you have achieved. Often, the things that make us stronger, are the things we dread the most.

We hope, by reading this book, that you now have the confidence and reassurance to deal with the challenges you face. It is your time to shine and be seen. Maintain your identity and self-esteem.

Tell yourself, '*I matter.*'

So, here are three questions that can help you focus on what you need to do to start recognising just what you can achieve with a positive attitude and mindset:

1. What would I have to believe about myself, in order to get what I want?
2. What would I need to commit to, to bring about the result I would like for myself, with or without my partner?
3. What goals would I like to achieve within the next six months, and who or what could help me do that?

This is your journey and you must make it one that works for you and leads to your ultimate happiness. Remember, there will be days when you feel you are back at the beginning; accept those days will happen. Keep The MAN*Script* in your handbag, desk drawer or wherever you will be able to easily pick it up for reassurance. It is there to help you on your daily personal journey.

You can't turn back time. You can't control what other people do, but you *can* control how you respond and you can make the right choices for yourself. You don't need to always consider others, you don't need to feel guilty for doing the things that make you feel better about yourself. You have to take responsibility for your future happiness and not leave it to others to decide that for you.

You may have started this book saying, "How COULD he do this to me?" We hope you now feel strong enough now to say, "How DARE he do this to me?"

And when you say it, really mean it.

YOU HAVE THE POWER, EMBRACE IT.

"Only you can control your future."

Dr Seuss,
American author, political cartoonist, poet, animator and
artist, 1904-1991

How to contact Julia and Jacqui

Contact us for further help and support, visit our website at:
www.keys2life.co.uk

Or email us personally at: hello@keys2life.co.uk

To help you through the recovery process we have developed the My Freedom Diary, available from summer 2018.

We have written The MAN*Script* specifically about the male-female relationship.

We are in the process of writing a book that speaks to men and same-sex relationships.

We would really welcome your thoughts and stories, so that we can all help each other.

Julia and Jacqui x